WeightWatchers®

Delicious recipes for all occasions

Chicken Favourites

First published in Great Britain by Simon & Schuster UK Ltd, 2012
A CBS Company

www.simonandschuster.co.uk

Simon & Schuster Australia, Sydney
Simon & Schuster India, New Delhi

Weight Watchers Publications: Cheryl Jackson, Jane Griffiths,
Selena Makepeace, Nina McKerlie and Imogen Prescott.

Recipes written by: Sue Ashworth, Sue Beveridge, Tamsin Burnett-Hall,
Cas Clarke, Siân Davies, Roz Denny, Nicola Graimes, Becky Johnson,
Kim Morphew, Joy Skipper, Penny Stephens and Wendy Veale as well
as Weight Watchers Leaders and Members.

Photography by: Iain Bagwell, Steve Baxter, Steve Lee, Juliet Piddington and
William Shaw.
Project editor: Nicki Lampon.
Design and typesetting: Geoff Fennell.

Colour reproduction by Dot Gradations Ltd, UK.
Printed and bound in China.

A CIP catalogue for this book is available from the British Library

ISBN 978-0-85720-935-1

1 2 3 4 5 6 7 8 9 10

Pictured on the title page: French roast chicken with boulangère potatoes p48.
Pictured on the Introduction: Huntsman chicken p100, Chicken fajitas with salsa p58,
Chicken with ratatouille p170.

WeightWatchers®

Delicious recipes for all occasions

Chicken Favourites

SIMON &
SCHUSTER
ILLUSTRATED

London · New York · Sydney · Toronto · New Delhi

A CBS COMPANY

Weight Watchers **ProPoints** Weight Loss System is a simple way to lose weight. As part of the Weight Watchers **ProPoints** plan you'll enjoy eating delicious, healthy, filling foods that help to keep you feeling satisfied for longer and in control of your portions.

Ⓥ This symbol denotes a vegetarian recipe and assumes that, where relevant, free range eggs, vegetarian cheese, vegetarian virtually fat free fromage frais, vegetarian low fat crème fraîche and vegetarian low fat yogurts are used. Virtually fat free fromage frais, low fat crème fraîche and low fat yogurts may contain traces of gelatine so they are not always vegetarian. Please check the labels.

❄ This symbol denotes a dish that can be frozen. Unless otherwise stated, you can freeze the finished dish for up to 3 months. Defrost thoroughly and reheat until the dish is piping hot throughout.

Recipe notes

Egg size: Medium, unless otherwise stated.

Raw eggs: Only the freshest eggs should be used. Pregnant women, the elderly and children should avoid recipes with eggs that are not fully cooked or raw.

All fruits and vegetables: Medium, unless otherwise stated.

Stock: Stock cubes are used in recipes, unless otherwise stated. These should be prepared according to packet instructions.

Recipe timings: These are approximate and meant to be guidelines. Please note that the preparation time includes all the steps up to and following the main cooking time(s).

Microwaves: Timings and temperatures are for a standard 800 W microwave. If necessary, adjust your own microwave.

Low fat spread: Where a recipe states to use a low fat spread, a light spread with a fat content of no less than 38% should be used.

Low fat soft cheese: Where low fat soft cheese is specified in a recipe, this refers to soft cheese with a fat content of less than 5%.

Contents

Introduction

Chicken – an incredibly versatile ingredient. From light bites to family favourites, speedy meals and special dishes for a dinner party, chicken is easy to cook and perfect in so many different recipes.

Add a few fresh ingredients for a wonderful Summer Chicken Casserole, rice for a zesty Lemon Chicken with Leeks and Rice or delicious spices for a Creamy Chicken Pasanda. Make Sunday special with a roast for family or friends, such as French Roast Chicken with Boulangère Potatoes, or treat yourself to a Thai Chicken Stir Fry just for you.

However you choose to cook chicken, you can't go wrong. It goes with anything and all these recipes are absolutely delicious and easy to follow. All you need to do is choose a recipe and get cooking your *Chicken Favourites*.

About Weight Watchers

For more than 40 years Weight Watchers has been helping people around the world to lose weight using a long term sustainable approach. Weight Watchers successful weight loss system is based on four tried and trusted principles:

- Eating healthily
- Being more active
- Adjusting behaviour to help weight loss
- Getting support in weekly meetings

Our unique *ProPoints* system empowers you to manage your food plan and make wise recipe choices for a healthier, happier you. To find out more about Weight Watchers and the *ProPoints* values for these recipes contact Customer Services on 0845 345 1500.

Storing and freezing

Many chicken dishes store well in the fridge, but make sure you use them up within a day or two. Some can also be frozen. However, it is important to make sure you know how to freeze safely.

- Wrap any food to be frozen in rigid containers or strong freezer bags. This is important to stop foods contaminating each other or getting freezer burn.
- Label the containers or bags with the contents and date – your freezer should have a star marking that tells you how long you can keep different types of frozen food.
- Never freeze warm food – always let it cool completely first.
- Never freeze food that has already been frozen and defrosted.
- Freeze food in portions, then you can take out as little or as much as you need each time.
- Defrost what you need in the fridge, making sure you put anything that might have juices, such as meat, on a covered plate or in a container.
- Fresh food, such as raw chicken, should be wrapped and frozen as soon as possible.
- Most fruit and vegetables can be frozen by open freezing. Lay them out on a tray, freeze until solid and then pack them into bags.
- Some vegetables, such as peas, broccoli and broad beans can be blanched first by cooking for 2 minutes in boiling water. Drain, refresh under cold water and then freeze once cold.

- Fresh herbs are great frozen – either seal leaves in bags or, for soft herbs such as basil and parsley, chop finely and add to ice cube trays with water. These are great for dropping into casseroles or soups straight from the freezer.

Some things cannot be frozen. Whole eggs do not freeze well, but yolks and whites can be frozen separately. Vegetables with a high water content, such as salad leaves, celery and cucumber, will not freeze. Fried foods will be soggy if frozen, and sauces such as mayonnaise will separate when thawed and should not be frozen.

Shopping hints and tips

Always buy the best ingredients you can afford. If you are going to cook healthy meals, it is worth investing in some quality ingredients that will really add flavour to your dishes. When buying meat, choose lean cuts of meat or lean mince, and if you are buying prepacked cooked sliced meat, buy it fresh from the deli counter.

When you're going around the supermarket it's tempting to pick up foods you like and put them in your trolley without thinking about how you will use them. So, a good plan is to decide what dishes you want to cook before you go shopping, check your store cupboard and make a list of what you need. You'll save time by not drifting aimlessly around the supermarket picking up what you fancy.

We've added a checklist here for some common store cupboard ingredients. Just add fresh ingredients in your regular shop and you'll be ready to cook your *Chicken Favourites*.

Store cupboard checklist

- ✓ apricot jam
- ☐ apricots, dried ready to eat
- ☐ artificial sweetener
- ✓ bay leaves
- ☐ black eyed beans, canned
- ☐ borlotti beans, canned
- ✓ breadcrumbs, natural dried
- ✓ brown sauce
- ✓ Cajun spice
- ☐ cannellini beans, canned
- ☐ cardamom pods
- ☐ chestnuts, canned
- ✓ chilli flakes
- ☐ chilli sauce
- ✓ Chinese five spice
- ✓ cinnamon sticks
- ✓ cinnamon, ground
- ✓ cloves
- ☐ coconut milk, reduced fat
- ✓ cooking spray, calorie controlled
- ✓ coriander seeds
- ✓ cornflour

- ☐ couscous, dried
- ✓ cumin, ground
- ✓ curry (paste and powder)
- ☐ fish sauce
- ✓ flour, plain
- ☐ garam masala
- ☐ harissa paste
- ✓ herbs, dried (mixed and Italian)
- ☐ honey, runny
- ☐ jerk seasoning
- ✓ kidney beans, canned
- ☐ lentils, dried red
- ☐ lime leaves, dried
- ☐ mayonnaise, extra light
- ✓ mixed spice
- ☐ mushrooms, dried porcini
- ✓ mustard (Dijon and wholegrain)
- ☐ noodles, dried
- ✓ oil (vegetable and olive)
- ☐ olives in brine, black
- ✓ paprika (regular and smoked)
- ✓ pasta, dried
- ✓ pearl barley, dried

- ☐ peppercorns
- ☐ pesto sauce
- ☐ pineapple, canned in natural juice
- ☐ pizza dough mix
- ☐ polenta, dried
- ☐ raisins
- ✓ rice, dried (basmati and long grain)
- ☐ rose water
- ✓ salt
- ☐ sesame seeds
- ✓ soy sauce
- ✓ stock cubes
- ✓ sugar, soft brown
- ☐ sweetcorn, canned
- ☐ tomato ketchup
- ✓ tomato purée
- ☐ tomatoes, canned
- ☐ turmeric
- ✓ vinegar (balsamic and wine) RED
- ☐ water chestnuts, canned
- ✓ Worcestershire sauce

Soups, salads and light bites

Thai chicken soup

Serves 4

235 calories per serving

Takes 20 minutes to prepare,
25 minutes to cook

1 teaspoon olive oil

1 lemongrass stem, chopped

1 cm (½ inch) fresh root
ginger, chopped finely

2 garlic cloves, crushed

330 g (11½ oz) skinless
boneless chicken breasts,
sliced into strips

1 small butternut squash,
peeled, de-seeded and diced

1 teaspoon Thai curry paste

850 ml (1½ pints) chicken
stock

3 tablespoons flaked almonds

100 ml (3½ fl oz) reduced fat
coconut milk

125 g (4½ oz) baby spinach,
washed

3 spring onions, sliced finely

salt and freshly ground black
pepper

*With the fragrant flavours of Thailand and the creaminess
of coconut milk, this soup is hard to resist.*

1 Heat the oil in a non stick saucepan and stir fry the lemongrass,
ginger and garlic for 2–3 minutes.

2 Add the chicken and stir fry for 5–6 minutes before adding
the butternut squash and Thai curry paste. Stir well to coat
the chicken and vegetables with the flavourings. Pour in the
chicken stock, bring to a simmer and cook for 15 minutes.

3 Meanwhile, dry fry the flaked almonds in a frying pan until
golden. Be careful not to let them burn.

4 Add the coconut milk, spinach and spring onions. Simmer
for a further 4–5 minutes to heat everything through and wilt
the spinach.

5 Season to taste and serve sprinkled with the toasted almonds.

Tip... The outer leaves of lemongrass can be very tough –
always remove a few layers before chopping or slicing
the inside.

Chunky chicken minestrone

Serves 4
127 calories per serving
Takes 10 minutes to prepare,
  20 minutes to cook
❄

**1.5 litres (2¾ pints) chicken
stock**
**2 x 100 g (3½ oz) skinless
boneless chicken breasts**
1 leek, sliced thinly
**1 carrot, peeled and grated
coarsely**
**a good pinch of dried mixed
herbs or dried thyme**
**30 g (1¼ oz) dried quick cook
macaroni or small soup
pasta shapes**
1 small courgette, chopped
105 g (3½ oz) garden peas
**a fresh basil sprig, torn
(optional)**
**salt and freshly ground black
pepper**

*This is a tasty and filling main meal soup. Make lots of it
and then freeze what you don't eat for a quick snack when
you are feeling hungry.*

1 Bring the stock to the boil in a large saucepan and carefully
add the chicken breasts, leek, carrot, dried herbs and seasoning.
Simmer for 15 minutes until the chicken is cooked. Remove the
chicken with a slotted spoon and set aside.

2 Stir the pasta, courgette and peas into the pan. Simmer for
a further 5 minutes until the pasta is tender.

3 Meanwhile, cut the chicken into small cubes. Return to the
soup and check the seasoning. Stir in the basil, if using, and
serve the soup in four warmed bowls.

Variation... Substitute 30 g (1¼ oz) of basmati rice for the
pasta, adding to the soup in step 3. Simmer for 10 minutes.

Chicken and lentil soup

Serves 4

140 calories per serving

Takes 10 minutes to prepare,
  25 minutes to cook

❄

**calorie controlled cooking
  spray**
1 large onion, chopped
2 celery sticks, chopped
**1.2 litre (2 pints) chicken
  stock**
2 garlic cloves, chopped
60 g (2 oz) dried red lentils
**250 g (9 oz) skinless boneless
  chicken breasts, cut into thin
  strips**
½ teaspoon Chinese five spice
**a handful of fresh coriander
  leaves, to garnish**

*Lentils are a very handy store cupboard ingredient. Use
them in soups and stews and for thickening sauces too.*

1 Spray a large lidded saucepan with the cooking spray and
heat until hot. Add the onion and celery and fry for 5 minutes,
adding a little stock if they start to stick. Stir in the garlic and
lentils followed by the remaining stock. Bring to the boil, cover
and simmer gently for 15 minutes.

2 Remove from the heat and liquidise until smooth using a
blender or hand held blender. Return to the pan to warm.

3 Meanwhile, toss the chicken in the Chinese five spice.
Spray a non stick frying pan with the cooking spray and heat
until hot. Add the chicken and cook, stirring occasionally, for
5 minutes until brown and cooked through.

4 Serve the soup in warmed bowls with the chicken on top
and garnished with the coriander.

Tip... If you like a hotter spice, add a pinch of chilli with the
Chinese five spice.

Thai style chicken salad

Serves 4
280 calories per serving
Takes 1 hour
❄ (chicken only)

4 x 75 g (2¾ oz) skinless
  boneless chicken thighs
1 tablespoon fish sauce
2 teaspoons finely diced red
  chilli
1 lemongrass stem, sliced
1 garlic clove, crushed
2 tablespoons lemon juice
2 teaspoons artificial
  sweetener
1 cucumber
110 g (4 oz) dried flat rice
  noodles
mixed leaves
salt

Marinating the chicken gives it extra flavour and salting the cucumber draws out the liquid making it deliciously crunchy.

1 Preheat the oven to Gas Mark 6/200°C/fan oven 180°C.

2 Place the chicken in a lidded, non metallic, ovenproof dish. Mix together the fish sauce, chilli, lemongrass, garlic, lemon juice and sweetener and pour over the chicken. Cover and leave at room temperature for 20 minutes.

3 Meanwhile, cut the cucumber into ribbons using a vegetable peeler. Sprinkle with salt and set aside for 10 minutes.

4 Roast the chicken, uncovered, in its dish for 30 minutes until golden and cooked through. Set aside to cool slightly and then cut into slices.

5 Bring a large saucepan of water to the boil, add the noodles and cook according to the packet instructions. Drain and keep warm.

6 Rinse the cucumber in cold water and pat dry with kitchen towel. Toss into the noodles with the mixed leaves and serve with the chicken.

Tip... Serve this salad warm or cold for lunch. If cooling and chilling for lunch, keep the leaves separate, otherwise they will wilt.

Devilled mushrooms with chicken

Serves 1
305 calories per serving
Takes 15 minutes

1 tablespoon Worcestershire sauce
1 teaspoon wholegrain mustard
½ teaspoon hot paprika
2 flat portobello mushrooms, wiped and stalks trimmed
calorie controlled cooking spray
50 g (1¾ oz) slice granary bread
1 tablespoon reduced fat mayonnaise
2 x 30 g (1¼ oz) slices cooked lean chicken
a small handful of wild rocket

This version of mushrooms on toast certainly has a wicked side. If you prefer it milder, just use normal paprika.

1 Preheat the grill to medium-high. In a small bowl, mix together the Worcestershire sauce, mustard and paprika. Put the mushrooms on a small baking tray and brush all over with the mixture. Spray with the cooking spray and set aside.

2 Put the granary bread under the grill and cook for 2 minutes, turning after 1 minute, until lightly toasted. Remove and set aside.

3 Transfer the marinated mushrooms to the grill and cook for 5 minutes until cooked through, turning after 2½ minutes.

4 Spread the toast with the mayonnaise and top with the sliced chicken, mushrooms and wild rocket. Serve immediately.

Chicken caesar salad

Serves 2

329 calories per serving

Takes 15 minutes to prepare
+ marinating, 10 minutes
to cook

**165 g (5¾ oz) skinless
boneless chicken breast,
cut into strips**

**1 tablespoon low fat natural
yogurt**

**2 teaspoons wholegrain
mustard**

**2 medium slices bread, crusts
removed and cubed**

1 Cos lettuce, chopped

**25 g (1 oz) Parmesan cheese
shavings**

**salt and freshly ground black
pepper**

For the dressing

**2 tablespoons reduced fat
houmous**

juice of ½ a lemon

*A classic recipe, this version includes chicken for a more
substantial meal.*

1 Place the chicken in a non metallic bowl with the yogurt and
mustard and season. Toss to coat and then leave to marinate
for as long as you can – from 30 minutes up to a few hours.

2 When ready to eat, preheat the grill to medium and toast the
bread on a baking tray until golden to make croûtons. Leave
the grill on a medium setting.

3 Divide the lettuce between two serving bowls and put the
dressing ingredients in a screw top jar with a tablespoon of
water. Shake well, pour over the lettuce and then toss together.
Sprinkle the croûtons over the top.

4 Grill the chicken on a baking tray or flameproof dish for
10 minutes, or until cooked through. Place on top of the salad
and scatter the Parmesan shavings over it. Serve immediately.

Lemon chicken salad wrap

Serves 1
283 calories per serving
Takes 12 minutes

100 g (3½ oz) skinless
boneless chicken mini fillets
or chicken breast, cut into
strips
calorie controlled cooking
spray
grated zest of ½ a lemon
1 teaspoon lemon juice
1 tablespoon low fat
mayonnaise
1 soft flour tortilla
15 g (½ oz) baby spinach,
washed
25 g (1 oz) cucumber, cut into
matchsticks
salt and freshly ground black
pepper

*Tortillas make a great alternative to sandwiches at
lunchtime. Extra tortillas can be individually wrapped
in cling film and frozen.*

1 Preheat the grill to a high setting.

2 Lightly season the chicken, mist with the cooking spray
and cook under the grill for 8–10 minutes, turning once, until
cooked through. Cut the chicken into chunky pieces

3 Meanwhile, mix the lemon zest, lemon juice and seasoning
with the mayonnaise. Warm the tortilla to soften it, either by
heating for 10–15 seconds on either side in a hot dry frying
pan, or by microwaving for 10 seconds.

4 Spread the lemon mayonnaise over the tortilla and scatter
the spinach, cucumber and chicken on top. Roll up and cut
in half to serve.

Tip... You can use 75 g (2¾ oz) of cold skinless cooked
chicken breast, sliced, skipping steps 1 and 2.

Chicken Waldorf salad

Serves 2
307 calories per serving
Takes 10 minutes

1 large red dessert apple,
  cored and sliced thinly
100 g (3½ oz) smoked or
  roasted skinless chicken,
  cubed
4 celery sticks, sliced thinly
½ small red cabbage,
  shredded thinly
30 g (1¼ oz) walnut pieces
150 g (5½ oz) mixed salad
  leaves
a small bunch of fresh chives,
  sliced finely, to garnish

For the dressing
1 teaspoon Dijon mustard
juice of an orange (about
  3 tablespoons)
2 tablespoons low fat
  mayonnaise

A Waldorf salad traditionally includes apples, celery and walnuts. It is named after the Waldorf Hotel in New York, where it was created.

1 Put all the salad ingredients, apart from the mixed leaves and chives, in a large bowl.

2 Shake all the dressing ingredients together in an empty jam jar with a screw top lid and then pour over the salad. Toss together. Arrange the mixed leaves on serving plates or in bowls and pile the salad on top.

3 Scatter with the chives and serve.

Warm sesame chicken salad

Serves 4
200 calories per serving
Takes 20 minutes

2 tablespoons stir fry oil or vegetable oil

350 g (12 oz) skinless boneless chicken breast, sliced into strips

4 celery sticks, sliced finely

1 red or yellow pepper, de-seeded and sliced finely

1 large carrot, peeled and cut into fine strips

1 small leek, sliced finely

2 teaspoons sesame seeds

1 tablespoon rice vinegar or white wine vinegar

a few drops of chilli sauce

4 generous handfuls of lamb's lettuce

salt and freshly ground black pepper

Colourful and tasty, the stir fry oil and chilli sauce in this recipe give it a little punch.

1 Heat 1 tablespoon of the oil in a wok or large non stick frying pan. Add the chicken and stir fry for 4–5 minutes, until browned and cooked.

2 Add the celery, pepper, carrot and leek to the wok or frying pan, stir fry for a further 1–2 minutes and then stir in the sesame seeds.

3 In a salad bowl, whisk together the remaining oil, vinegar and chilli sauce. Season.

4 Add the lamb's lettuce, chicken and vegetables to the salad bowl. Toss together and serve at once.

Tip... Stir fry oil is flavoured with ginger, garlic and spices, and it gives an excellent flavour to this recipe.

Variation... If you can't find lamb's lettuce, use watercress or young spinach leaves instead.

Curried chicken pasta salad lunchbox

Serves 1
448 calories per serving
Takes 20 minutes

60 g (2 oz) dried pasta twists
calorie controlled cooking
  spray
100 g (3½ oz) skinless
  boneless chicken breast
½ teaspoon curry powder
a pinch of turmeric
1 teaspoon lemon juice
30 g (1¼ oz) low fat soft
  cheese
125 g (4½ oz) low fat natural
  yogurt
1 teaspoon artificial sweetener
½ red, yellow or orange
  pepper, de-seeded and diced
2 spring onions, chopped
  roughly
2 tablespoons chopped fresh
  coriander

Substantial salads are ideal for lunch, whether you eat at home or at work. This mildly spiced pasta salad will keep you going all afternoon.

1 Bring a saucepan of water to the boil, add the pasta and cook for 10–12 minutes or according to the packet instructions. Drain and rinse in cold water.

2 Meanwhile, spray a non stick frying pan with the cooking spray and cook the chicken breast for 5 minutes on each side or until cooked through. Remove from the pan, allow to cool and then slice.

3 Mix the curry powder, turmeric and lemon juice together to make a paste. Blend in the soft cheese until smooth. Add the yogurt and sweetener and mix together well.

4 Stir in the remaining ingredients, including the pasta and chicken, until everything is well coated in the dressing. Transfer to a lunchbox, seal and chill until ready to serve.

Chicken liver pâté with melba toast

Serves 6

174 calories per serving

Takes 20 minutes +
    30 minutes chilling

25 g (1 oz) low fat spread
2 banana shallots, chopped
1 garlic clove, chopped
**350 g (12 oz) chicken livers,
    rinsed and dried on kitchen
    towel**
1½ tablespoons tomato purée
1½ tablespoons brandy
**6 medium slices white bread,
    crusts removed**

*Pâté is quick and easy to make and this version is tasty
and healthier too.*

1 Melt the low fat spread in a small pan and, when hot, add
the shallots. Cook, stirring, for 3–4 minutes. Add the garlic and
continue cooking for another 2 minutes until softened. Add the
chicken livers and sauté for 5 minutes. Stir in the tomato purée
and brandy.

2 Remove from the heat and cool slightly. Transfer to a food
processor, or use a hand held blender, and blend until smooth.
Spoon into six individual small ramekins or serving dishes and,
when cool, cover and chill for 30 minutes.

3 To make the melba toast, preheat the grill to medium. Cut
through each piece of bread horizontally to make two slices.
Cut each of these into two triangles and then toast under the
grill on one side. Serve warm with the pâté.

**Tip... You can make the pâté up to 24 hours in advance,
cover and chill until required.**

Sticky chicken bites

Serves 2

222 calories per serving

Takes 40 minutes +
   30 minutes marinating

❄

300 g (10½ oz) skinless
   boneless chicken breasts,
   cut into bite size pieces

2 tablespoons tomato ketchup

2 tablespoons dark soy sauce

½ teaspoon Chinese five spice

1 teaspoon runny honey

2 celery sticks, sliced thinly

1 carrot, peeled and sliced
   thinly

*Little morsels of tasty chicken that are just right for a light
meal or snack.*

1 Place the chicken in a shallow dish. Mix together the ketchup,
soy sauce, Chinese five spice and honey and drizzle it over the
chicken. Mix well, cover and leave to marinate for 30 minutes.

2 Preheat the oven to Gas Mark 5/190°C/fan oven 170°C.
Line a baking tray with non stick baking parchment.

3 Mix the celery and carrot with the chicken and then arrange
the coated pieces on the baking tray. Bake for 25 minutes, until
the chicken is cooked through and the marinade has formed a
sticky glaze.

Crunchy Parmesan chicken

Serves 2

296 calories per serving

Takes 10 minutes to prepare,
  15 minutes to cook

❄ (raw only)

25 g (1 oz) dried polenta

1 teaspoon mustard powder

25 g (1 oz) Parmesan cheese,
  grated

1 egg, beaten

300 g (10½ oz) skinless
  boneless chicken breasts,
  cut into even bite size
  chunks

freshly ground black pepper

*Finger lickin' good. These golden nuggets are especially
good with a large salad of Little Gem lettuce leaves,
tomatoes, cucumber, peppers and radishes.*

1 Preheat the oven to Gas Mark 6/200°C/fan oven 180°C and
put a non stick baking tray in to heat.

2 Mix together the polenta, mustard powder, Parmesan and
freshly ground black pepper and put into a bowl. Put the beaten
egg into another bowl.

3 Put the chicken chunks first in the beaten egg to coat and
then spoon them into the polenta mixture. Stir until all the
pieces are coated. You can be quite rough. Remove the baking
tray from the oven, transfer the chicken to the tray and bake
for 15 minutes until golden and cooked. Serve immediately.

Curried chicken parcels

Makes 8 parcels

151 calories per serving

Takes 25 minutes to prepare,
15 minutes to cook

❄

140 g (5 oz) carrots, peeled
and diced

200 g (7 oz) potatoes, peeled
and diced

calorie controlled cooking
spray

300 g (10½ oz) skinless
boneless chicken breasts,
chopped finely

2 spring onions, chopped

50 g (1¾ oz) frozen peas

1 tomato, chopped

2 teaspoons medium curry
powder

4 x 45 g (1½ oz) filo pastry
sheets, measuring
50 x 24 cm (20 x 9½ inches),
defrosted if frozen

1 tablespoon sunflower oil

salt and freshly ground black
pepper

These spiced pasties are great for lunch or a snack.

1 Preheat the oven to Gas Mark 5/190°C/fan oven 170°C.
Bring a lidded saucepan of water to the boil, add the carrots
and potatoes, cover, cook until tender and then drain.

2 Meanwhile, lightly spray a non stick frying pan with the
cooking spray, add the chicken and spring onions and stir fry
over a high heat for 4 minutes, stirring to break up the chicken.

3 Add the peas, tomato, curry powder and drained vegetables
and fry for 2 minutes, lightly mixing the ingredients. Season
and transfer to a plate to cool.

4 Cut the sheets of filo pastry in half lengthways, into eight
long strips. Working with one strip at a time, brush lightly with
sunflower oil and spoon one eighth of the filling near to one
end. Bring the corner near the filling across to the other side to
make a triangle enclosing the filling. Keep folding the pastry up
and round until you have an enclosed triangular parcel. Place
on a non stick baking tray, sprayed with the cooking spray.
Repeat with the rest of the filling and pastry strips.

5 Bake for 15 minutes until crisp and golden brown. Serve
warm or at room temperature.

Tzatziki chicken pittas

Serves 2
306 calories per serving
Takes 30 minutes +
  marinating

50 g (1¾ oz) low fat natural
  yogurt
75 g (2¾ oz) 0% fat Greek
  yogurt
1 tablespoon chopped fresh
  mint
½ teaspoon dried mint
1 small garlic clove, crushed
2 x 100 g (3½ oz) skinless
  boneless chicken breasts
4 cm (1½ inches) cucumber,
  diced
2 wholemeal pitta breads
1 large tomato, sliced
salad leaves, to serve

These Greek-style pittas are a tasty alternative to a kebab.
The longer the chicken is marinated before cooking, the
more the flavour will develop.

1 Mix the two types of yogurt together with the fresh mint,
dried mint and garlic. Set half of the mixture aside to make
the tzatziki and pour the other half into a plastic food bag.

2 Using a sharp knife, cut four shallow slashes in the top
of each chicken breast and place in the bag with the yogurt
mixture. Squeeze out the excess air and seal. Place the bag
in the fridge and leave to marinate for at least 30 minutes.

3 Mix the diced cucumber into the reserved yogurt mixture
and chill the tzatziki until ready to serve.

4 Preheat the grill to medium. Remove the chicken from its
marinade and cook under the grill for 7–8 minutes on each
side. The juices should run clear when the thickest part of the
breast is pierced with a skewer.

5 Place the chicken on a clean chopping board and let it rest
for 5 minutes. Warm the pitta breads under a medium grill
(or in the toaster) for 45–60 seconds on each side.

6 Slice the chicken and transfer to a warmed serving plate.
Split the pittas open, spoon in some tzatziki and fill with the
chicken and tomato slices. Serve with the salad leaves.

Tip... Fresh and dried mint give very different flavours to
this recipe, but if you don't have any fresh mint to hand
you can simply increase the dried mint to 1 teaspoon.

Chicken kebabs with herb and garlic dipping sauce

Serves 1
282 calories per serving
Takes 15 minutes + 1 hour
marinating

juice of ½ a lime
2 teaspoons soft brown sugar
½ teaspoon paprika
**150 g (5½ oz) skinless
boneless chicken breast,
cut into bite size pieces**

For the dipping sauce
**60 g (2 oz) low fat soft cheese
with garlic and herbs**
2 tablespoons skimmed milk
**salt and freshly ground black
pepper**

*Fun to make and a great meal for one. Serve with a mixed
salad and 60 g (2 oz) of dried long grain rice, cooked
according to the packet instructions.*

1 In a small bowl, mix together the lime juice, sugar and
paprika. Stir in the chicken and set aside to marinate for
1 hour.

2 Soak two wooden kebab sticks in water (this stops them
from burning during cooking). If you don't have wooden kebab
sticks, use metal skewers. Preheat the grill to high.

3 Thread 4–6 pieces of chicken on to each kebab stick and
grill for 6–8 minutes, turning after 4 minutes.

4 Meanwhile, whisk the soft cheese and skimmed milk
together, until you have a smooth sauce. Season to taste.
Serve with the kebabs.

Variation... You can vary the dipping sauce by substituting
other low fat soft cheeses for the herb and garlic one used
here.

Soy-glazed chicken livers

Serves 4
192 calories per serving
Takes 20 minutes

1 tablespoon sunflower oil
2 garlic cloves, crushed
350 g (12 oz) chicken livers,
halved, rinsed and dried on
kitchen towel
1 tablespoon cornflour
1 teaspoon Chinese five spice
3 tablespoons soy sauce
1 tablespoon runny honey
1 tablespoon sherry
1 tablespoon tomato purée
fresh salad leaves, to serve

Chicken livers are relatively inexpensive and take very little preparation and cooking. Try out this recipe; it may become a firm favourite.

1 Heat the sunflower oil in a large non stick frying pan and fry the garlic for a few seconds.

2 Toss the chicken livers with the cornflour and Chinese five spice. Add to the pan and stir fry for 5 minutes. Don't overcook or they'll toughen up.

3 Mix together the soy sauce, honey, sherry and tomato purée. Add to the pan. Cook until the juices bubble and then spoon on to a bed of crisp fresh salad leaves. Serve at once.

Chicken satay

Serves 4

153 calories per serving

Takes 15 minutes to prepare
+ 1 hour marinating,
10–12 minutes to cook

**200 g (7 oz) skinless boneless
chicken breast, thinly sliced**

For the marinade

**½ tablespoon ground
cinnamon**
½ tablespoon ground cumin
50 ml (2 fl oz) soy sauce
freshly ground black pepper

For the satay sauce

**1 teaspoon Thai green curry
paste**
**2 tablespoons reduced fat
coconut milk**
**½ tablespoon muscovado
sugar**
**40 g (1½ oz) peanuts, chopped
finely**

*A deliciously nutty and spicy chicken dish – great for
summer barbecues.*

1 Mix together the marinade ingredients in a non metallic bowl.
Place the strips of chicken in the marinade, cover with cling film
and leave to marinate for at least 1 hour. Light the barbecue, if
using, or preheat the grill to hot.

2 Thread the chicken strips on to eight kebab skewers and pour
over the remaining marinade.

3 In a small saucepan, mix together the satay sauce ingredients
with 2 tablespoons of water. Bring to a simmer and continue to
simmer until thickened – this takes about 2 minutes.

4 Meanwhile, place the chicken sticks on the barbecue or under
a hot grill and cook for 10–12 minutes, turning occasionally until
the chicken is cooked.

5 Serve the chicken sticks with the satay sauce poured over or
in a side dish, ready to dip into.

Tip... If you are using wooden kebab sticks always soak
them in cold water for 30 minutes before using them. This
will prevent them from burning.

Chicken drumsticks with gremolata

Serves 4

200 calories per serving

Takes 20 minutes to prepare,
   25 minutes to cook

❄

8 x 75 g (2¾ oz) chicken
   drumsticks, skinned
1 tablespoon lemon juice
½ teaspoon paprika

For the gremolata
15 g (½ oz) fresh flat leaf
   parsley, chopped very finely
1 garlic clove, crushed
finely grated zest and juice of
   ½ a lemon
2 shallots, chopped very finely
1 teaspoon clear honey
1 teaspoon olive oil
salt and freshly ground black
   pepper

*Keep a tub of the zesty sauce in the fridge; it will last for
3 days and is wonderful served with grilled meats.*

1 Preheat the oven to Gas Mark 5/190°C/fan oven 170°C.
Line a baking tray with non stick baking parchment. Make
2–3 diagonal slits along the top of each chicken drumstick.
Lay them on the baking tray.

2 Mix together the lemon juice and paprika and brush a little
over each drumstick. Roast for 25 minutes, until the chicken
is cooked through.

3 Mix together all the ingredients for the gremolata. Serve the
cooked chicken with a spoonful of gremolata each

Variation... Use a teaspoon of sesame oil instead of olive oil
to add a different flavour to the gremolata.

Family favourites

French roast chicken with boulangère potatoes

Serves 4

532 calories per serving as suggested

Takes 15 minutes to prepare, 1 hour 15 minutes to cook

1.75 kg (4 lb) whole chicken
½ lemon
1 onion, thickly sliced
650 ml (23 fl oz) chicken stock
1 garlic clove, crushed
2 tablespoons chopped fresh tarragon
salt and freshly ground black pepper
a small bunch of watercress, to garnish (optional)

For the boulangère potatoes
1 kg (2 lb 4 oz) potatoes, peeled and sliced thinly
1 onion, sliced thinly
calorie controlled cooking spray
300 ml (10 fl oz) skimmed milk

1 Preheat the oven to Gas Mark 5/190°C/fan oven 170°C. Wipe the chicken inside and out with kitchen towel, tuck the lemon half inside and season. Place the sliced onion in a small roasting tin and sit the chicken on top, breast side down.

2 Roast for 45 minutes and then turn the chicken breast side up and cook for a further 20–30 minutes. The juices should run clear when the thickest part of the leg is pierced.

3 As soon as the chicken is in the oven, lightly spray an ovenproof baking dish with the cooking spray and layer the potato and onion slices in it, seasoning as you go. Pour the milk and 500 ml (18 fl oz) of chicken stock over, spray a sheet of foil with the cooking spray and place on top.

4 Bake in the oven for 1–1½ hours, removing the foil for the last 10 minutes so that the potatoes can brown. The potatoes can be kept warm if they are ready before the chicken.

5 When the chicken is ready, remove to a platter, cover with foil, and leave to rest for 10 minutes before carving. This will give a juicier, more moist chicken.

6 Place the roasting tin on the hob, using an oven glove to hold it, and add the remaining stock, garlic and tarragon. Bring to a simmer, stirring to release the caramelised chicken juices from the tin, and bubble gently for 5 minutes.

7 Carve the chicken thinly, removing the skin, and serve three 50 g (1¾ oz) slices each with the tarragon gravy and boulangère potatoes. Garnish with the watercress, if using.

Lemon chicken burger

Serves 4

398 calories per serving

Takes 20 minutes to prepare,
  15 minutes to cook

❄ (chicken only)

**4 x 125 g (4½ oz) skinless
  boneless chicken breasts**

**grated zest and juice of
  2 lemons**

**125 g (4½ oz) natural dried
  breadcrumbs**

**2 tablespoons finely chopped
  fresh curly parsley**

1 egg, beaten

1 tablespoon plain flour

**calorie controlled cooking
  spray**

**2 x 50 g ciabatta rolls, cut
  in half**

1 teaspoon garlic purée

**2 tablespoons reduced fat
  mayonnaise**

2 tablespoons soured cream

**1 tablespoon snipped fresh
  chives**

*Burgers are the ultimate in comfort food and the whole
family will love them. Fill the bun with lots of lettuce, sliced
gherkins, tomatoes and onion.*

1 Preheat the oven to Gas Mark 6/200°C/fan oven 180°C.
Put a non stick baking tray in to heat.

2 With each piece of chicken, make a large horizontal cut
from the right side through the middle but leaving it still
attached. Open up like a book. Put into a shallow dish and
squeeze over the lemon juice. Set aside.

3 In a separate shallow dish, mix together the breadcrumbs,
lemon zest and parsley. Put the beaten egg in another dish.
Dust the chicken with the flour, dip it into the egg and then
into the breadcrumbs, until coated all over.

4 Preheat the grill to hot. (If your grill is in your oven and not
separate, toast the rolls first, before cooking the chicken.)
Remove the baking tray from the oven, spray the chicken with
the cooking spray and put on to the preheated baking tray.
Cook the chicken in the oven for 12–15 minutes until golden.

5 Meanwhile, grill the ciabatta halves for 1–2 minutes.
Combine the garlic, mayonnaise, soured cream and chives.
Serve the chicken on a roll half, topped with mayonnaise.

Farmhouse chicken casserole

Serves 4

202 calories per serving

Takes 30 minutes to prepare,
1 hour to cook

❄

calorie controlled cooking
spray

450 g (1 lb) skinless boneless
chicken breasts, cut into bite
size chunks

1 onion, chopped

225 g (8 oz) carrots, peeled
and sliced

350 g (12 oz) potatoes, peeled
and diced

4 celery sticks, sliced

1 tablespoon wholegrain
mustard

225 g (8 oz) cooking apple,
peeled, cored and diced

25 g (1 oz) dried pearl barley

150 ml (5 fl oz) medium dry
cider

300 ml (10 fl oz) chicken stock

2 fresh thyme sprigs or
1 teaspoon dried thyme

salt and freshly ground black
pepper

*This wholesome classic casserole is given a hint of
sweetness with an apple.*

1 Heat a large, lidded, flameproof casserole dish or large,
lidded, non stick pan and spray with the cooking spray. Add
the chicken and stir fry for 2–3 minutes until it is sealed on
all sides.

2 Add the onion, carrots, potatoes and celery to the dish or
pan and cook for 2 minutes. Stir in the mustard, apple, pearl
barley, cider and stock.

3 Season to taste, add the thyme and bring to the boil. Reduce
the heat and cover. Simmer for 1 hour, stirring occasionally,
until the pearl barley is tender and the apple has cooked to a
pulp, thickening the sauce.

Chicken and mushroom bake

Serves 4

342 calories per serving

Takes 15 minutes to prepare,
30 minutes to cook

15 g (½ oz) dried porcini
mushrooms

600 ml (20 fl oz) hot vegetable
or chicken stock

calorie controlled cooking
spray

4 x 150 g (5½ oz) skinless
boneless chicken breasts

2 garlic cloves, crushed

3 x 400 g cans borlotti beans,
drained and rinsed

450 g (1 lb) chestnut
mushrooms, sliced thickly

a few fresh thyme sprigs,
woody stems removed,
chopped roughly

1 teaspoon dried oregano or
marjoram

salt and freshly ground black
pepper

a handful of fresh parsley,
chopped, to garnish
(optional)

A beautiful autumnal dish that is filling and tasty too.

1 Put the porcini mushrooms in a jug with the hot stock and leave to infuse for a few minutes.

2 Preheat the oven to Gas Mark 4/180°C/fan oven 160°C.

3 Spray a large non stick frying pan with the cooking spray. Place the chicken breasts in the frying pan, season and brown on both sides. Remove them to a plate and then stir fry the garlic for a few seconds in the same pan.

4 Add a little of the stock from the soaking mushrooms and scrape up any bits stuck to the bottom of the pan.

5 Put the beans and chestnut mushrooms in a roasting tin, add the stock and garlic from the pan, and the stock and dried mushrooms from the jug, scatter with the thyme and oregano or marjoram and stir.

6 Arrange the chicken breasts on top, cover with foil and bake in the oven for 25 minutes. Remove the foil and brown for a further 10 minutes. Scatter with fresh parsley, if using, and serve.

Glazed chicken with winter mash

Serves 4
385 calories per serving
Takes 30 minutes

4 x 25 g (1 oz) smoked streaky bacon rashers

4 x 165 g (5¾ oz) skinless boneless chicken breasts

2 tablespoons pomegranate molasses

2 teaspoons red wine vinegar

4 tablespoons brown sauce

4 carrots, peeled and sliced

500 g (1 lb 2 oz) parsnips, peeled and cut into chunks

2 leeks, sliced thinly

salt and freshly ground black pepper

Serve with a selection of green vegetables such as mange tout and sugar snap peas.

1 Wrap a bacon rasher around the middle of each chicken breast and then put in a shallow dish. In a jug, mix together the pomegranate molasses, vinegar and brown sauce. Pour this over the chicken to coat and set aside.

2 Preheat the grill to medium-high. Bring a large lidded saucepan of water to the boil, add the carrots, bring back to the boil and simmer, covered, for 5 minutes.

3 Meanwhile, remove the chicken from the marinade and put on a foil lined baking tray. Cook for 15–20 minutes under the grill, turning halfway through cooking, until the juices run clear.

4 Add the parsnips to the carrots and simmer for a further 3 minutes. Finally, add the leeks and simmer for 2 minutes until all the vegetables are tender. Drain and then return to the pan and mash thoroughly. Season generously and serve immediately with the chicken.

Tip... Pomegranate molasses is the result of reducing pomegranate juice until it is really thick and syrupy and it has a sweetly tart taste. You'll find it in most large supermarkets or Middle Eastern shops.

Chicken Kiev

Serves 4

288 calories per serving

Takes 20 minutes to prepare,
35–40 minutes to cook

❄

calorie controlled cooking
    spray
4 x 150 g (5½ oz) skinless
    boneless chicken breasts
125 g (4½ oz) low fat soft
    cheese with garlic and herbs
1 egg
2 tablespoons plain flour
50 g (1¾ oz) fresh white
    breadcrumbs
salt and freshly ground black
    pepper

*Serve with 100 g (3½ oz) low fat chips per person and
vegetables such as fine green beans, cauliflower or
carrots.*

1 Preheat the oven to Gas Mark 5/190°C/fan oven 170°C.
Spray a non stick baking tray with the cooking spray.

2 Put the chicken breasts, well spaced apart, between sheets
of cling film or greaseproof paper. Use a meat mallet or rolling
pin to beat them out until flattened, but avoid bashing them
until they break up. Remove the cling film or paper.

3 Divide the soft cheese into four equal portions. Place the
cheese portions on the chicken breasts, towards the wider end
of the chicken, and season. Roll up the breasts, folding in the
sides to encase the cheese. Use cocktail sticks to secure them.

4 Beat the egg in a small bowl with 2 tablespoons of cold
water. Roll the chicken parcels in the flour and then dip them
in the beaten egg mixture. Finally, roll them in the breadcrumbs
and place them on the baking tray.

5 Bake for 35–40 minutes, until golden brown and thoroughly
cooked. To check, pierce the chicken with a skewer or sharp
knife – the juices should run clear. Remove the cocktail sticks
before serving.

Variation... For an extra garlic hit, spread ½ teaspoon of
garlic purée over each chicken breast before adding the
cheese.

Chicken fajitas with salsa

Serves 4
280 calories per serving
Takes 15 minutes

2 large tomatoes, chopped
¼ cucumber, chopped finely
1 small red onion, chopped finely
2 tablespoons chopped fresh coriander or mint
2 teaspoons lime or lemon juice
4 soft flour tortillas
175 g (6 oz) cooked skinless boneless chicken breast, torn into strips
4 tablespoons half fat crème fraîche
25 g (1 oz) extra mature half fat Cheddar cheese, grated
salt and freshly ground black pepper

If you are feeling very hungry, serve these with 30 g (1¼ oz) of dried white rice per person, cooked according to the packet instructions.

1 Preheat the oven to Gas Mark 2/150°C/fan oven 130°C or preheat the grill to medium.

2 To make the salsa, mix together the tomatoes, cucumber, onion and coriander or mint. Add the lime or lemon juice and season.

3 Warm the tortillas in the oven or under the grill for 3–4 minutes.

4 Lay out the warm tortillas and spoon on some salsa. Divide the cooked chicken between them. Top with the crème fraîche and sprinkle with the grated cheese, dividing the total amounts between the four tortillas. Roll up and serve with the remaining salsa.

Chicken calzone

Serves 4

355 calories per serving

Takes 25 minutes to prepare
+ rising, 10–15 minutes to
cook

245 g packet pizza dough mix
2 teaspoons dried oregano
calorie controlled cooking
spray
200 g (7 oz) skinless boneless
chicken breast, diced
1 small red onion, chopped
1 tablespoon plain flour, for
dusting
125 g (4½ oz) mozzarella light,
chopped
3 tomatoes, chopped roughly
a handful of fresh basil leaves
1 egg white, beaten lightly
salt and freshly ground black
pepper
green salad, to serve

A calzone is a folded pizza, with the filling on the inside.

1 Make up the pizza dough according to the packet instructions, stirring in the oregano before adding the water. Cover and leave in a warm place until doubled in size, while you make the filling.

2 Spray a non stick frying pan with the cooking spray and heat until hot. Add the chicken pieces and onion and stir fry for 5–7 minutes until brown and cooked through. Set aside to cool a little.

3 Preheat the oven to Gas Mark 7/220°C/fan oven 200°C. Dust a work surface with ½ a tablespoon of flour. Divide the dough into four and roll each into a circle approximately 15 cm (6 inches) in diameter. Top one half of each circle with a quarter of the chicken mixture and a quarter of the cheese, tomatoes and basil. Season and brush around the edge with the egg white. Fold over the dough to create a semi circle and squeeze together the edges to seal. Repeat to make four calzone in total.

4 Dust a non stick baking tray with the remaining flour, transfer all the calzone to the tray and brush the tops with the remaining egg white. Bake for 10–15 minutes until golden and puffed up. Serve warm with the salad on the side.

Cheesy chicken with butternut chips

Serves 4

320 calories per serving

Takes 10 minutes to prepare,
30 minutes to cook

**800 g (1 lb 11 oz) butternut
squash, peeled and
de-seeded**

**calorie controlled cooking
spray**

**75 g (2¾ oz) mild soft goat's
cheese**

**1 tablespoon snipped fresh
chives**

**4 x 150 g (5½ oz) skinless
boneless chicken breasts**

4 slices Parma ham

freshly ground black pepper

*Soft goat's cheese has a mild tangy flavour but, if you
prefer, you can use the same amount of low fat soft cheese
with herbs instead.*

1 Preheat the oven to Gas Mark 6/200°C/fan oven 180°C.

2 Cut the squash into finger width chips. Spread out on a large
non stick baking tray and lightly coat with the cooking spray.
Season with freshly ground black pepper and then in the oven
for 10 minutes.

3 In a bowl, mix the goat's cheese with the chives. Cut a
pocket in the thickest part of each chicken breast and spoon
in the cheese mixture. Tuck a slice of Parma ham over each
chicken breast, covering up the pocket of stuffing.

4 Remove the baking tray from the oven and add the chicken
breasts to the tray, stirring the butternut squash chips around.
Cook in the oven for a further 20 minutes, until the chicken is
cooked through and the chips are tender and beginning
to brown.

Chicken, leek and sweetcorn cobbler

Serves 4
404 calories per serving
Takes 20 minutes to prepare,
20 minutes to cook

calorie controlled cooking spray
400 g (14 oz) skinless boneless chicken breasts, diced
2 leeks, sliced
25 g (1 oz) plain flour
300 ml (10 fl oz) chicken stock
150 ml (5 fl oz) skimmed milk, plus 1 teaspoon to glaze
150 g (5 ½ oz) frozen sweetcorn

For the cobbler

150 g (5½ oz) self raising flour
a pinch of salt
60 g (2 oz) low fat spread
1 tablespoon snipped fresh chives
4 tablespoons low fat natural yogurt
freshly ground black pepper

A savoury cobbler makes a delicious change from the traditional pastry topped pie. The cobbler topping is essentially a savoury scone mixture. Serve with carrots and green cabbage.

1 Preheat the oven to Gas Mark 4/180°C/fan oven 160°C. Heat a non stick frying pan until hot and spray with the cooking spray. Cook the chicken for 3 minutes until starting to brown and then add the leeks and cook for another 2 minutes.

2 Stir the flour in to coat the chicken and leeks and then gradually blend in the stock and milk. Bring to the boil and simmer for 5 minutes. Stir the sweetcorn into the sauce and then pour the filling into an ovenproof dish.

3 To make the cobbler, reserve 1 tablespoon of the flour for rolling out and sift the rest into a mixing bowl with a pinch of salt. Season with black pepper and, using your fingertips, rub in the low fat spread. Stir in the chives and then add the yogurt to bind to a soft but not sticky dough, adding a little water if needed.

4 Dust the work surface with the reserved flour and pat the dough out to 1 cm (½ inch) thick. Stamp out 12 x 5 cm (2 inches) rounds using a cutter, re-rolling as needed, and place on top of the chicken filling. Brush with 1 teaspoon of milk to glaze and bake in the oven for 20 minutes until the cobbler topping is risen and golden brown.

Chicken and chestnut stew

Serves 4

332 calories per serving

Takes 15 minutes to prepare,
1 hour 10 minutes to cook

calorie controlled cooking
 spray

**450 g (1 lb) skinless boneless
 chicken thighs**

225 g (8 oz) shallots, peeled

**225 g (8 oz) button, field or
 chestnut mushrooms, halved**

**200 g (7 oz) vacuum packed or
 canned cooked chestnuts**

400 ml (14 fl oz) chicken stock

2 bay leaves

2 tablespoons tomato purée

**salt and freshly ground black
 pepper**

Serve with steamed green cabbage.

1 Heat a large, lidded, flameproof pan or casserole dish and
spray with the cooking spray.

2 Add the chicken thighs and shallots and cook over a high
heat for 5 minutes, turning the chicken until it is browned on
all sides.

3 Add the mushrooms, chestnuts, stock, bay leaves, tomato
purée and seasoning and stir.

4 Reduce the heat, cover and simmer over a low heat for
1 hour.

Chicken lasagne

Serves 4

435 calories per serving

Takes 45 minutes to prepare,
  25 minutes to cook

❄

2 teaspoons olive oil

350 g (12 oz) skinless
  boneless chicken breasts,
  cut into bite size chunks

450 g (1 lb) leeks, sliced thinly

1 garlic clove, crushed

400 g can chopped tomatoes

2 tablespoons tomato purée

1 teaspoon dried basil

150 ml (5 fl oz) boiling water

8 no precook lasagne sheets

300 ml (10 fl oz) skimmed milk

25 g (1 oz) cornflour

200 g (7 oz) low fat soft
  cheese

25 g (1 oz) Parmesan cheese,
  grated

salt and freshly ground black
  pepper

A lighter version of the traditional lasagne.

1 Heat the oil in a non stick frying pan and add the chicken, leeks and garlic. Stir fry for 5 minutes until the chicken begins to brown.

2 Add the chopped tomatoes, tomato purée, basil and boiling water and season. Simmer for 15 minutes.

3 Preheat the oven to Gas Mark 5/190°C/fan oven 170°C.

4 Spoon half the chicken and leek mixture into a deep, ovenproof, rectangular dish, and then arrange four sheets of lasagne on top. Spoon on the remaining chicken mixture and finish with the last four lasagne sheets.

5 Heat the milk until it is boiling. In a bowl, mix the cornflour to a thin paste with a little cold water. Pour the boiling milk into the bowl and then return this mixture to a clean pan and cook, whisking, until it thickens. Stir in the soft cheese and then pour the cheese sauce over the top of the lasagne sheets.

6 Sprinkle the surface of the lasagne with the Parmesan and bake in the oven for 25 minutes.

Tip... Lasagne is always a good standby meal to have at hand. It freezes well, so wrap up any leftovers in individual portions and pop them in the freezer for another day.

Roast chicken with autumn fruits

Serves 4

283 calories per serving

Take 10 minutes to prepare,
35 minutes to cook

25 g (1 oz) plain flour

**2 teaspoons sage and apple
seasoning or dried mixed
herbs**

**4 x 165 g (5¾ oz) skinless
boneless chicken breasts**

1 tablespoon olive oil

2 apples

1 pear

1 tablespoon lemon juice

**salt and freshly ground black
pepper**

*Chicken is coated in sage and apple seasoning and then
roasted with apples and pears. This is a great recipe for
the whole family and ideal for Sunday lunch.*

1 Preheat the oven to Gas Mark 5/190°C/fan oven 170°C.

2 Sprinkle the flour on to a plate and add the sage and apple
seasoning or mixed herbs. Season and mix well.

3 Rinse the chicken breasts, but do not pat dry. Roll in the
seasoned flour. Place in a roasting tin, sprinkle with the oil,
transfer to the oven and cook for 15 minutes.

4 Quarter and core the apples and pear, without peeling them.
Sprinkle with the lemon juice and place them next to the
chicken. Roast for a further 20 minutes, or until the chicken
is cooked and the fruit is tender.

Variations... Use garlic flavoured olive oil if you like; it adds
a delicious taste to the chicken.

If you want to use a whole chicken, brush the chicken
with olive oil and then roll in the seasoned flour in step 2.
Sprinkle the chicken with 1 teaspoon of oil and then cook
in the oven for 1 hour, or until the juices run clear when the
thickest part of the bird is pierced.

Lemon chicken pasta

Serves 4

586 calories per serving

Takes 10 minutes to prepare,
50 minutes to cook

**4 teaspoons wholegrain
mustard**

2 tablespoons runny honey

**4 x 165 g (5¾ oz) skinless
boneless chicken breasts**

**1 garlic bulb, broken into
cloves but not peeled**

**4 red onions, cut into eight
wedges**

**leaves from 4 fresh rosemary
sprigs**

1 lemon, quartered

300 ml (10 fl oz) chicken stock

350 g (12 oz) dried pasta

**salt and freshly ground black
pepper**

*Chicken breasts are roasted with lemon, garlic and
rosemary and tossed with pasta to make this robust
country-style dish.*

1 Preheat the oven to Gas Mark 6/200°C/fan oven 180°C.

2 Mix together the mustard and honey and spread on top of
each chicken breast. Place the chicken in a roasting tin with
the garlic cloves, onion wedges and rosemary leaves. Squeeze
over the lemon juice and place the leftover lemon peel in the
tray too. Pour over the stock and season.

3 Cover the tin with foil and place in the oven for 45 minutes.
Remove the foil and cook for a further 5 minutes.

4 Meanwhile, bring a saucepan of water to the boil, add the
pasta and cook according to the packet instructions. Drain.

5 Remove the lemon peel from the roasting tin and discard.
Remove the chicken, slice and keep warm. Remove the garlic
cloves, peel and return to the tin with the cooked pasta. Toss
the pasta with the vegetables and juices in the tray and serve
on warmed plates topped with a sliced chicken breast.

Chicken and broccoli pie

Serves 4

430 calories per serving

Takes 40 minutes to prepare,
20 minutes to cook

❄

700 g (1 lb 9 oz) potatoes,
peeled and diced

1 tablespoon wholegrain
mustard

2 tablespoons 0% fat Greek
yogurt

25 g (1 oz) low fat spread

25 g (1 oz) plain flour

300 ml (10 fl oz) skimmed milk

350 g (12 oz) broccoli, broken
into florets

400 g (14 oz) cooked skinless
boneless chicken breasts,
cubed

50 g (1¾ oz) half fat Red
Leicester cheese, grated

salt and freshly ground black
pepper

A simple pie topped with mashed potato that will go down well with all the family.

1 Bring a saucepan of water to the boil, add the potatoes and cook for 15 minutes until tender. Drain and mash thoroughly with the mustard and yogurt.

2 Meanwhile, melt the low fat spread in a small saucepan and stir in the flour. Cook, stirring, for 1 minute and then gradually add the milk. Stir until you have a smooth thickened sauce. Season to taste and simmer for 2 minutes.

3 Preheat the oven to Gas Mark 5/190°C/fan oven 170°C. Bring a second saucepan of water to the boil, add the broccoli florets and cook for 2 minutes only. Drain thoroughly.

4 Mix the chicken into the sauce along with the broccoli and grated cheese and stir well. Spoon the mixture into an ovenproof dish and top with the mashed potatoes – using the prongs of a fork to mark a pattern on the top of the mash.

5 Bake for 20 minutes, until piping hot, and serve straight away.

Tip... Don't overcook the broccoli or it will go very mushy and lose its attractive colour.

Chicken and mushroom stroganoff

Serves 4

183 calories per serving

Takes 25 minutes to prepare,
 25 minutes to cook

❄

**calorie controlled cooking
 spray**
1 onion, sliced
1 garlic clove, crushed
350 g (12 oz) skinless
 boneless chicken breasts,
 cut into thin strips
225 g (8 oz) button
 mushrooms, sliced
1 teaspoon paprika
1 tablespoon Worcestershire
 sauce
2 tablespoons brandy
1 chicken stock cube
300 ml (10 fl oz) boiling water
100 g (3½ oz) half fat crème
 fraîche
2 tablespoons chopped fresh
 parsley
salt and freshly ground black
 pepper

*Stroganoff is traditionally made with beef, but this lighter
version is every bit as tasty. It's great served with fine
green beans or mange tout to add a burst of colour to
the dish.*

1 Heat a large non stick frying pan and spray with the cooking
spray. Add the onion and garlic, reduce the heat and cook gently
for 5 minutes until the onion has softened, but not browned.
Add the chicken to the pan and stir fry for 5 minutes until it is
sealed on all sides.

2 Add the mushrooms, paprika, Worcestershire sauce and brandy
and cook, stirring, for 2 minutes. Crumble the stock cube into
the pan and add the boiling water. Bring to the boil and then
reduce the heat and simmer, uncovered, for 20 minutes, stirring
from time to time.

3 Add the crème fraîche and parsley and season. Stir well and
heat through gently for 2 minutes – don't allow it to boil and
bubble as the sauce may separate.

Chicken goulash with dumplings

Serves 4

330 calories per serving

Takes 25 minutes to prepare,
45 minutes to cook

calorie controlled cooking
  spray

4 x 150 g (5½ oz) skinless
  boneless chicken breasts

1 onion, chopped finely

2 leeks, chopped

2 celery sticks, chopped

3 garlic cloves, crushed

2 tomatoes, chopped roughly

a small bunch of fresh thyme,
  tough stems removed and
  leaves and tender stems
  chopped

600 ml (20 fl oz) vegetable or
  chicken stock

1 bay leaf

1 teaspoon paprika

salt and freshly ground black
  pepper

For the dumplings

1 egg, beaten

250 g (9 oz) cottage cheese

50 g (1¾ oz) dried polenta

*These fantastic light dumplings are made with cottage
cheese and polenta. They are the perfect accompaniment
to this delicious stew.*

1 Make the dumplings first by stirring the egg into the cottage
cheese and then gently folding in the polenta and seasoning.
Cover and chill for at least 20 minutes.

2 For the goulash, heat a large flameproof casserole dish and
spray with the cooking spray. Season the chicken and fry on
both sides until golden brown.

3 Add the onion, leeks, celery, garlic, tomatoes, thyme, stock
and bay leaf. Bring to the boil and simmer for 45 minutes.

4 Meanwhile, using wet hands, shape the dumpling mixture
into eight golf-ball sized dumplings.

5 Stir the paprika into the stew and then gently place the
dumplings on top. Cover, steam for a further 5–10 minutes
and then serve.

Tandoori chicken with minty mango raita

Serves 4
258 calories per serving
Takes 30 minutes +
marinating

2 garlic cloves, crushed
2.5 cm (1 inch) fresh root
ginger, grated finely
2 teaspoons turmeric
2 teaspoons garam masala
2 teaspoons coriander seeds,
crushed
250 g (9 oz) low fat natural
yogurt
juice of ½ a lemon
400 g (14 oz) skinless
boneless chicken breasts,
cut into thick strips
lime wedges, to serve
(optional)

For the minty mango raita
1 large mango, peeled, stoned
and cut into small cubes
½ small onion, grated
½ cucumber, diced finely
1 teaspoon brown mustard
seeds
a small bunch of fresh mint,
chopped finely
250 g (9 oz) low fat natural
yogurt

This tandoori is not the lurid pink you may be used to.
That's because it doesn't have any chemical colourants
in it and, consequently, is much better for you.

1 Mix the garlic, ginger, spices, yogurt and lemon juice together
in a freezer bag. Add the chicken and toss until covered. Seal
the bag and chill for at least 30 minutes, or up to overnight.

2 Meanwhile, make the raita by mixing together all the
ingredients and chilling.

3 Preheat the oven to Gas Mark 7/220°C/fan oven 200°C.
Remove the chicken from the freezer bag and place in a non
stick roasting tin. Roast for 20 minutes, until cooked through
and browned on the edges.

4 Serve with the raita and lime wedges, if using.

Chicken, potato and chorizo roast

Serves 4

320 calories per serving

Takes 10 minutes to prepare,
50 minutes to cook

1 tablespoon smoked paprika

4 x 185 g (6½ oz) chicken
breast quarters, skin
removed

350 g (12 oz) potatoes, peeled
and cubed

2 preserved lemons from a
jar, drained and sliced

2 garlic cloves, sliced

100 ml (3½ fl oz) hot chicken
stock

50 g (1¾ oz) thin chorizo
slices

2 tablespoons finely chopped
fresh flat leaf parsley, to
garnish

*Relax and enjoy this fabulous roast for longer on those lazy
Sunday afternoons – there's hardly any washing up to do,
only one roasting tin.*

1 Preheat the oven to Gas Mark 5/190°C/fan oven 170°C.
Rub the paprika all over the chicken breast quarters and then
put them into a deep roasting tin along with the potato cubes,
preserved lemons and garlic. Pour over the stock and roast in
the oven for 30 minutes.

2 Remove the roasting tin from the oven and scatter over
the chorizo slices. Return to the oven and roast for a further
15–20 minutes until the potatoes are tender and the chicken
is cooked (the juices should run clear when a skewer is
inserted). Sprinkle with the parsley and serve.

Variation... If you can't find chicken breast quarters, you
can use 4 x 100 g (3½ oz) skinless chicken drumsticks and
4 x 85 g (3 oz) skinless chicken thighs.

Dishes with spice

Aromatic chicken curry

Serves 2
515 calories per serving
Takes 15 minutes to prepare,
   30–35 minutes to cook
❄

1 tablespoon vegetable oil
1 onion, chopped finely
1 garlic clove, crushed
3 cm (1¼ inches) fresh root
   ginger, grated finely
½ teaspoon turmeric
½ teaspoon ground cumin
½ teaspoon ground coriander
¼ teaspoon chilli powder
¼ teaspoon garam masala
2 ripe tomatoes, chopped
350 g (12 oz) boneless
   skinless chicken breasts, cut
   into bite size pieces
150 ml (5 fl oz) chicken stock
2 tablespoons half fat crème
   fraîche
salt and freshly ground black
   pepper

*This recipe has all the strong fabulous flavours of Indian
food. Serve with 60 g (2 oz) of dried basmati rice per
person, cooked according to the packet instructions.*

1 Heat the oil in a large non stick saucepan, add the onion
and garlic and fry for about 5 minutes until softened. Add the
ginger and spices and fry for a further minute.

2 Add the tomatoes, chicken and stock. Bring to the boil
and then turn down the heat. Simmer on a medium heat for
20 minutes, until the sauce is thick and rich.

3 Turn off the heat and stir in the crème fraîche. Check the
seasoning and serve.

Tips... The curry tastes more fragrant if you use whole
spices like coriander and cumin seeds. Grind the spices
in a pestle and mortar or electric grinder just before you
use them.

You can prepare the curry in advance until step 3. Keep it
in the refrigerator or freezer and then reheat and add the
crème fraîche when you want to eat it.

Stuffed Moroccan chicken

Serves 6
196 calories per serving
Takes 30 minutes
❄ (up to step 3 before cooking)

6 x 150 g (5½ oz) skinless boneless chicken breasts
calorie controlled cooking spray
50 g (1¾ oz) raisins
½ teaspoon ground mixed spice
1 teaspoon rose harissa paste
1 preserved lemon, pips removed and chopped finely
3 tablespoons fresh breadcrumbs
1 tablespoon finely chopped fresh parsley

Serve with tomatoes on the vine and 60 g (2 oz) of dried couscous per person, cooked according to the packet instructions and mixed with herbs and a squeeze of lemon.

1 Preheat the oven to Gas Mark 5/190°C/fan oven 170°C and put a baking tray in to heat.

2 Cut a pocket into the thickest part of each chicken breast using a small sharp knife. Heat a large non stick frying pan until hot. Spray the chicken breasts with the cooking spray and then cook the chicken for 3–4 minutes until brown all over. Remove and set aside.

3 In a bowl, mix together the raisins, mixed spice, harissa paste, lemon, breadcrumbs and parsley. Use to fill each chicken pocket – don't worry if it squidges out.

4 Remove the baking tray from the oven, transfer the chicken to the tray, spray with the cooking spray and bake in the oven for 20 minutes or until the juices run clear. Serve immediately.

Tip... Preserved lemons are a Moroccan ingredient. If you can't find them, then use the grated zest of a large lemon.

Chicken saag aloo

Serves 4

354 calories per serving

Takes 25 minutes to prepare,
20 minutes to cook

❄

calorie controlled cooking
spray

4 x 150 g (5½ oz) skinless
boneless chicken breasts,
cubed

200 g (7 oz) small new
potatoes, quartered

1 onion, chopped finely

4 garlic cloves, crushed

5 cm (2 inches) fresh root
ginger, chopped finely

400 g can chopped tomatoes

300 g (10½ oz) frozen spinach

300 ml (10 fl oz) chicken stock

2 tablespoons tandoori or balti
curry paste

a bunch of fresh coriander,
chopped

salt and freshly ground black
pepper

lemon wedges, to serve

A simple quick curry that takes advantage of the delicious curry pastes that you can buy in jars. Serve with a tomato and shredded onion salad.

1 Heat a large non stick frying pan and spray with the cooking spray. Add the chicken and stir fry the chicken for 4 minutes or so until golden on the edges and white all over. Add the potatoes, onion, garlic and ginger and stir fry for a further 4 minutes.

2 Add the tomatoes, spinach, stock and curry paste and bring to the boil. Simmer gently for 20 minutes, until the chicken is tender, the potatoes cooked through and the sauce thickened.

3 Stir in the coriander and check the seasoning, adding more if necessary. Serve with the lemon wedges.

Chicken pilaff

Serves 2

470 calories per serving

Takes 10 minutes to prepare,
  20 minutes to cook

❄

calorie controlled cooking
  spray

3 spring onions, chopped

½ small green pepper,
  de-seeded and chopped

1 small carrot, peeled and
  grated coarsely

2 teaspoons garlic purée

150 g (5½ oz) skinless
  boneless chicken breast,
  cubed

1 teaspoon mild or medium
  curry powder

150 g (5½ oz) dried easy cook
  basmati rice

400 ml (14 fl oz) chicken stock

100 g (3½ oz) frozen peas

salt and freshly ground black
  pepper

2 tablespoons low fat natural
  yogurt, to serve

This is a great one pot meal as the meat, vegetables and rice are all cooked together. Use easy cook basmati rice for its special flavour. If you are cooking this just for yourself, save half and freeze it for another day.

1 Heat a large, lidded, non stick saucepan and spray with the cooking spray. Add the spring onions, pepper, carrot, garlic purée and 4 tablespoons of water, cook until the mixture sizzles and then cover and simmer for 3 minutes.

2 Remove the lid and stir the chicken into the pan along with the curry powder. Heat for 1 minute or so until the meat is sealed, stirring once or twice.

3 Add the rice and then stir in the stock and seasoning. Bring to the boil, stirring. Reduce the heat, cover the pan and cook for 15 minutes until the liquid is absorbed and the chicken is cooked.

4 Mix in the peas, check the seasoning and reheat for 2 minutes until the peas are piping hot. Serve the pilaff on two warmed plates, each topped with a tablespoon of yogurt.

Thai red chicken curry

Serves 4
234 calories per serving
Takes 30 minutes

4 dried lime leaves (optional)

¼ kettleful of boiling water

150 g (5½ oz) baby corn, sliced

150 g (5½ oz) sugar snap peas

calorie controlled cooking spray

350 g (12 oz) skinless boneless chicken breasts, diced

6 spring onions, cut into thirds

200 ml (7 fl oz) reduced fat coconut milk

200 ml (7 fl oz) chicken stock

1 teaspoon light brown soft sugar

110 g (4 oz) cherry tomatoes, halved

chopped fresh coriander, to garnish

For the red curry paste

½ red onion

1 red chilli, de-seeded and sliced

1 small lemongrass stem, sliced thinly

grated zest and juice of ½ a lime

2.5 cm (1 inch) fresh root ginger, sliced

1 garlic clove

1 tablespoon fish sauce

Serve with 60 g (2 oz) of dried basmati rice per person, cooked according to the packet instructions.

1 Place the curry paste ingredients in a food processor or blender and blend until finely chopped.

2 Soak the lime leaves (if using) in boiling water for 5 minutes and then cut into fine shreds.

3 Bring a saucepan of water to the boil, add the baby corn and sugar snap peas and cook for 3 minutes. Drain and set aside.

4 Spray a wok or large non stick frying pan with the cooking spray and stir fry the chicken and spring onions for 3 minutes. Add the curry paste and stir fry for 1 minute.

5 Blend in the coconut milk and chicken stock and then add the shredded lime leaves (if using), sugar and blanched vegetables. Simmer gently for 3 minutes and then add the cherry tomatoes and cook for 2 minutes before ladling into warmed bowls. Garnish with the coriander.

Tip... If you want, use 2 tablespoons of ready made Thai red curry paste instead.

Variation... To make green Thai curry paste, substitute a green chilli for the red one and a regular onion for the red one, and add 2 tablespoons of chopped fresh coriander.

Jamaican jerk chicken

Serves 2

506 calories per serving

Takes 10 minutes to prepare,
25–30 minutes to cook

❄

**calorie controlled cooking
spray**

1 tablespoon dried polenta

**½ tablespoon Jamaican jerk
seasoning**

1 small egg white

**2 x 165 g (5¾ oz) skinless
boneless chicken breasts**

**75 g (2¾ oz) dried long grain
rice**

**200 g (7 oz) canned kidney
beans, drained and rinsed**

a kettleful of boiling water

**salt and freshly ground black
pepper**

To serve

chopped fresh parsley

2 tomatoes, quartered

*Enjoy the exotic flavours of the Caribbean in this easy
recipe.*

1 Preheat the oven to Gas Mark 6/200°C/fan oven 180°C.
Spray a roasting tin with the cooking spray.

2 On a large plate, mix the polenta with the jerk seasoning
and seasoning.

3 Beat the egg white with 2 teaspoons of water and brush
all over the chicken, then toss the chicken in the seasoning
mixture to coat it on all sides. Place the chicken in the roasting
tin and bake it in the oven for 25–30 minutes, until it is tender.

4 When the chicken has been in the oven for 15 minutes,
bring a saucepan of water to the boil, add the rice and cook
for about 12 minutes, or according to the packet instructions,
adding the kidney beans for the final 3–4 minutes to heat
them through.

5 Drain the rice and beans and rinse them with boiling water.
Divide the rice mixture between two warmed serving plates
and place the chicken on top. Sprinkle with plenty of fresh
parsley and serve with the tomatoes.

Tip... Look out for Jamaican jerk seasoning in the spice
racks or speciality food section of your local supermarket.
It is quite fiery, so add a little at a time, according to your
taste.

Mexican chicken with spicy salsa

Serves 2

364 calories per serving

Takes 20 minutes +
marinating

2 x 150 g (5½ oz) skinless
boneless chicken breasts

grated zest and juice of 2
limes

½ teaspoon chilli powder or
crushed dried chilli flakes

½ teaspoon dried oregano or
marjoram

a small bunch of fresh
coriander, chopped

calorie controlled cooking
spray

salt and freshly ground black
pepper

For the salsa

1 mango, skinned, stoned and
diced

1 small red chilli, de-seeded
and chopped finely

½ small red onion, chopped
finely

3 tomatoes, quartered,
de-seeded and chopped

An easy light chicken dish that could be served with a
225 g (8 oz) potato per person, baked in its skin.

1 Sprinkle the chicken with the lime zest and juice, chilli,
oregano or marjoram and half the coriander. Season and leave
to marinate for a few minutes (1 hour would be preferable).

2 Meanwhile, mix together all the salsa ingredients with the
remaining coriander. Season and place in a serving bowl.

3 Preheat the grill to high or heat a non stick griddle pan.
Spray the chicken with the cooking spray. Grill under the hot
grill or on the griddle for 4–5 minutes on each side until cooked
through and golden on the outside. The juices should run clear
when the chicken is pierced with a skewer in the thickest part.
Serve with the salsa.

Spicy barley chicken

Serves 6
337 calories per serving
Takes 20 minutes to prepare,
 1 hour 5 minutes to cook

6 x 165 g (5¾ oz) skinless
 boneless chicken breasts,
 each cut into three pieces on
 the diagonal
calorie controlled cooking
 spray
1 onion, chopped roughly
2 garlic cloves, chopped
1 teaspoon turmeric
1 teaspoon ground cumin
1 teaspoon ground coriander
200 g (7 oz) dried pearl barley
600 ml (20 fl oz) chicken stock
150 g (5½ oz) cherry
 tomatoes, halved
25 g packet fresh coriander,
 leaves chopped
salt and freshly ground black
 pepper

Originally from the Middle East, pearl barley is a husked and polished grain, with an almost nutty flavour. You can find it in most supermarkets near the lentils and other grains.

1 Heat a large, lidded, non stick saucepan and spray the chicken with the cooking spray. Cook the chicken pieces for 5 minutes until brown. You may need to do this in batches.

2 Return all the chicken to the pan. Add the onion and garlic and cook for 3–4 minutes until starting to soften.

3 Add the turmeric, cumin and ground coriander and cook for 1 minute, stirring. Add the pearl barley and chicken stock. Bring to the boil. Cover and simmer for 1 hour until the juices have nearly all been absorbed and the barley is tender.

4 Stir through the tomatoes and half the coriander and cook for 3–4 minutes until just soft. Check the seasoning and then top with the remaining coriander and serve immediately in bowls.

Cajun chicken

Serves 2
541 calories per serving
Takes 15 minutes to prepare,
  25 minutes to cook

2 teaspoons Cajun spice
4 x 75 g (2¾ oz) chicken
  drumsticks, skin removed
calorie controlled cooking
  spray
125 g (4½ oz) dried couscous
150 ml (5 fl oz) chicken stock
40 g (1½ oz) peas, defrosted
198 g can sweetcorn, drained
2 spring onions, chopped
grated zest and juice of a lime
salt and freshly ground black
  pepper

Chicken drumsticks dusted with Cajun spices make a tasty meal.

1 Preheat the oven to Gas Mark 6/200°C/fan oven 180°C.

2 Sprinkle the spice over the drumsticks, ensuring they are evenly coated. Spray generously with the cooking spray and bake in a non stick roasting tin for 25 minutes until golden and cooked through. When a skewer is inserted, the juices should run clear.

3 Place the couscous and stock in a lidded pan and bring to the boil. Take off the heat, cover with a tight fitting lid and leave to steam. After 10 minutes, fluff up the couscous with a fork and stir in the peas, sweetcorn, spring onions and lime zest and juice. Season.

4 Serve the drumsticks on a bed of the couscous.

Tip... If you prefer, cook all the ingredients, leave to cool and chill to enjoy as a salad. It makes a great lunchbox meal too.

Oriental chicken

Serves 4

342 calories per serving

Takes 15 minutes to prepare,
25 minutes to cook

150 g (5½ oz) dried brown
basmati rice

2 x 5 g sushi nori seaweed
sheets, torn into large pieces

2 teaspoons Chinese five spice

4 x 165 g (5¾ oz) skinless
boneless chicken breasts

calorie controlled cooking
spray

8 radishes, trimmed and
grated

50 g (1¾ oz) beansprouts

1 small Chinese leaf lettuce,
shredded finely

25 g packet fresh coriander,
leaves chopped

1 tablespoon sushi rice
seasoning

juice of a lime

*Sushi nori is paper thin toasted sheets of seaweed and is
available from most supermarkets or Oriental shops. It is
usually used in Japanese cooking for wrapping sushi.*

1 Preheat the oven to Gas Mark 4/180°C/fan oven 160°C.
Bring a saucepan of water to the boil, add the rice and simmer
for 20–25 minutes until tender or according to the packet
instructions.

2 Meanwhile, in a small food processor, whizz the seaweed
and Chinese five spice until chopped roughly. Transfer to a
shallow bowl and roll each chicken breast in the mixture
to coat.

3 Transfer the chicken breasts to a non stick baking tray, spray
with the cooking spray and bake in the oven for 20–25 minutes
until cooked and the juices run clear. Remove from the oven,
loosely cover with foil and set aside for 5 minutes.

4 Meanwhile, in a large salad bowl mix together the radishes,
beansprouts, Chinese leaf lettuce, coriander, sushi rice
seasoning and lime juice.

5 Drain the rice, stir into the salad bowl until combined and
then divide between four plates. Slice the chicken into thick
slices on the diagonal and serve on top of each rice salad.

Huntsman chicken

Serves 4

264 calories per serving

Takes 20 minutes to prepare,
30 minutes to cook

❋

4 x 150 g (5½ oz) skinless
boneless chicken breasts

4 x 25 g (1 oz) lean back
bacon rashers

1 tablespoon finely chopped
fresh flat leaf parsley, to
garnish

For the barbecue sauce

calorie controlled cooking
spray

20 silverskin onions, drained
and rinsed

1 garlic clove, crushed

1 tablespoon light brown soft
sugar

2 tablespoons cider vinegar

1 tablespoon tomato ketchup

2 teaspoons Dijon mustard

1 teaspoon mild chilli powder

1 tablespoon tomato purée

1 tablespoon brown sauce

*Serve with 150 g (5½ oz) cooked potato, mashed with
1 tablespoon of skimmed milk, carrots, shredded spring
greens and broccoli.*

1 Preheat the oven to Gas Mark 5/190°C/fan oven 170°C.

2 To make the barbecue sauce, heat a non stick saucepan
and spray with the cooking spray. Cook the onions and garlic
for 3–4 minutes until lightly browned. Add the remaining
ingredients and 125 ml (4 fl oz) of water and bring to the boil.
Simmer for 5 minutes until beginning to thicken. Set aside.

3 Wrap each chicken breast with a rasher of bacon and put
into an ovenproof dish. Pour over the barbecue sauce and
bake in the oven for 30 minutes until cooked. Sprinkle with
the parsley and serve.

Chicken biryani

Serves 4
448 calories per serving
Takes 40 minutes to prepare,
  50 minutes to cook

For the rice

calorie controlled cooking
spray

4 cloves

4 cm (1½ inch) cinnamon stick

2 garlic cloves, crushed

4 cm (1½ inches) fresh root
ginger, grated

300 g (10½ oz) dried basmati
rice, rinsed and drained

For the chicken

350 g (12 oz) skinless
boneless chicken breasts,
cut into bite size pieces

150 g (5½ oz) low fat natural
yogurt

1 teaspoon ground cumin

1 teaspoon chilli powder

1 teaspoon turmeric

calorie controlled cooking
spray

2 onions, chopped

400 g can chopped tomatoes

2 teaspoons garam masala

salt and freshly ground black
pepper

To serve (optional)

a small bunch of fresh
coriander or mint

1 teaspoon rose water

A fabulous and satisfying supper.

1 Heat a saucepan and spray with the cooking spray. Add the cloves, cinnamon, garlic and ginger and fry for 1 minute. Add the rice and 600 ml (20 fl oz) of water, bring to the boil and simmer for 25 minutes until most of the water has been absorbed. Cover and cook for a further 5 minutes and then turn off the heat and set aside.

2 Meanwhile, mix the chicken with the yogurt, cumin, chilli powder and turmeric, season and set aside.

3 Heat a large non stick pan and spray with the cooking spray. Add the onions and stir fry until softened and then add the tomatoes and garam masala and cook for 10 minutes. Add the chicken mixture and 300 ml (10 fl oz) of hot water.

4 Bring to the boil and simmer for 20 minutes until the sauce is thick and the chicken is cooked through.

5 Preheat the oven to Gas Mark 6/200°C/fan oven 180°C. Layer the chicken and rice in a deep ovenproof dish, finishing with a rice layer, and bake for 10 minutes.

6 To serve, sprinkle with fresh coriander or mint and the rose water, if using.

Spicy chicken and black eyed bean stew

Serves 4

432 calories per serving

Takes 15 minutes to prepare,
  20 minutes to cook

❄

calorie controlled cooking
  spray

**600 g (1 lb 5 oz) skinless
  boneless chicken thighs,
  diced**

1 large onion, chopped roughly

**1½ green peppers, de-seeded
  and chopped roughly**

¼ teaspoon hot chilli powder

400 g can chopped tomatoes

**410 g can black eyed beans,
  drained and rinsed**

**salt and freshly ground black
  pepper**

**150 g (5½ oz) 0% fat Greek
  yogurt, to serve**

A hearty spicy stew that is perfect with broccoli.

1 Heat a large, lidded, flameproof casserole and spray with the cooking spray. Brown the chicken for 5–6 minutes over a high heat and then remove to a plate.

2 Spray the casserole again with the cooking spray and cook the onion and peppers for 4 minutes. Stir in the chilli powder and chicken and then add the chopped tomatoes and beans. Season, cover and simmer for 20 minutes.

3 Serve the stew topped with the yogurt, in warmed bowls.

Thai green chicken with coconut sauce

Serves 2
400 calories per serving
Takes 15 minutes

75 g (2¾ oz) dried easy cook rice

225 g (8 oz) broccoli, broken into small florets

50 g (1¾ oz) sugar snap peas or green beans, trimmed

225 g (8 oz) skinless boneless chicken breast, cut into strips

4 spring onions, chopped

2 tablespoons Thai green curry paste

100 ml (3½ fl oz) reduced fat coconut milk

1 tablespoon chopped fresh coriander

salt and freshly ground black pepper

Green curry paste is a delicious blend of green peppers, green chillies, lemongrass, coriander, fish sauce, garlic and lime juice.

1 Bring a saucepan of water to the boil, add the rice and cook according to the packet instructions.

2 Meanwhile, bring a second saucepan of water to the boil and cook the broccoli for 5 minutes. Add the sugar snap peas or green beans and cook for a further 2 minutes. Make sure that the vegetables still have some 'bite'.

3 Dry fry the chicken strips in a non stick pan until golden. Stir in the spring onions and curry paste and cook for a further minute. Add the drained vegetables, coconut milk and coriander. Heat gently, combining the ingredients. Season to taste.

4 Serve the curry on a bed of rice.

Tips... If you have ever wondered what the difference is between red and green curry paste, red curry paste is milder and sweeter.

If you have any coconut milk left over, simply freeze it in ice cube trays and then pop out 2 cubes per serving for an instant curry.

Spicy mango chicken pancakes

Makes 6 pancakes
287 calories per serving
Takes 25 minutes

127 g packet pancake batter mix

1 egg

calorie controlled cooking spray

500 g jar Homepride Curry Cook-in Sauce

450 g (1 lb) cooked skinless boneless chicken breasts, chopped

1 ripe mango, peeled, stoned and chopped

2 spring onions, chopped

3 firm tomatoes, sliced

Serve this unusual dish with a crisp green salad.

1 Make the pancake batter according to the packet instructions, adding the egg. Spray a small non stick omelette pan or frying pan with the cooking spray and heat gently. Add a spoonful or two of batter to the pan, cook for 1–2 minutes until bubbles appear and then turn over and cook until golden brown. Repeat to make six pancakes. Wrap the cooked pancakes in foil and keep warm under a low grill setting.

2 Gently heat the curry sauce in a saucepan and add the cooked chicken. Heat thoroughly, stirring, until piping hot.

3 Fold in the mango pieces and spring onion. Divide the filling between the pancakes. Fold into neat squares, and arrange on a foil lined grill pan. Top each pancake with slices of tomato.

4 Heat through under the grill until the tomatoes are lightly cooked and the pancakes are hot.

Cheat's chicken makhani

Serves 2
269 calories per serving
Takes 20 minutes

230 g can chopped tomatoes
1 teaspoon tomato purée
1 teaspoon grated fresh root
  ginger
2 garlic cloves, crushed
¼ teaspoon hot chilli powder
200 ml (7 fl oz) chicken stock
15 g (½ oz) ground almonds
1 teaspoon caster sugar
225 g (8 oz) chicken tikka
  pieces
1 tablespoon half fat butter
½ teaspoon garam masala

This cheat's version of chicken makhani (butter chicken)
is fabulously rich tasting. Stirring in a little butter at the
end enriches the sauce wonderfully, so don't leave it out.
Accompany with a plain mini naan bread per person, to
mop up the flavoursome sauce.

1 Place the chopped tomatoes, tomato purée, ginger, garlic,
chilli powder and chicken stock in a saucepan. Simmer briskly,
uncovered, for 10 minutes to reduce.

2 Stir in the ground almonds, sugar and chicken tikka pieces.
Gently heat through for 7 minutes and then stir in the butter
and garam masala. Serve straight away.

Chicken piri piri

Serves 2
446 calories per serving
Takes 35 minutes

2 small red chillies, de-seeded and chopped

a small bunch of fresh tarragon, chopped

a small bunch of fresh basil, chopped

1 bay leaf

2 tablespoons raisins

2 tablespoons lemon juice

1 tablespoon olive oil

1 kg (2 lb 4 oz) skinless whole poussin or spring chicken

salt and freshly ground black pepper

fresh parsley sprigs, to serve (optional)

Piri piri seasoning is a mixture of chillies and citrus peel originating in Portuguese Africa. Serve this dish with 60 g (2 oz) of dried long grain rice per person, cooked according to the packet instructions, and lemon wedges.

1 Make the piri piri marinade by putting all the ingredients except the chicken and parsley sprigs in a bowl and leaving to infuse for 5 minutes.

2 Split the chicken down the back, but don't separate the two halves completely. Press it out flat on a board using a weight if necessary. Fix with crossed skewers to maintain the shape during grilling

3 Preheat the grill to high and brush the chicken inside and out with the marinade. Place the chicken under the grill, skin side down, and cook for 10 minutes, basting frequently with the marinade. Turn the chicken over and cook the other side for 10 minutes until cooked through, again basting frequently.

4 To serve, slice 160 g (5¾ oz) per person, garnished with the parsley sprigs, if using.

Tip... Spatchcock chicken or poussin gets its name from the way it is flattened out and skewered. It is available from supermarkets or you could ask your butcher to prepare one for you.

Creamy chicken pasanda

Serves 2
361 calories per serving
Takes 35 minutes
❄

**calorie controlled cooking
  spray**
1 onion, chopped finely
2 cardamom pods, split
**2.5 cm (1 inch) fresh root
  ginger, chopped finely**
2 garlic cloves, chopped finely
½ teaspoon chilli powder
1 teaspoon turmeric
1 teaspoon ground coriander
**300 g (10½ oz) skinless
  boneless chicken breasts,
  cubed**
**300 ml (10½ fl oz) chicken
  stock**
**6 tablespoons 0% fat Greek
  yogurt**
2 tablespoons ground almonds
6 cherry tomatoes, halved
**salt and freshly ground black
  pepper**

This is just as tasty as a takeaway curry.

1 Spray a lidded non stick saucepan with the cooking spray.
Add the onion and cook, covered, for 7 minutes until softened.

2 Add the cardamom pods, ginger, garlic, spices and chicken
and stir fry for about 5 minutes or until the chicken is coloured.
Add a little water from time to time if the mixture looks dry.

3 Pour in the stock, bring to the boil, reduce the heat and
simmer, covered, for 8 minutes.

4 Gradually add the yogurt and, when it is all mixed in, stir in
the ground almonds and cherry tomatoes. Replace the lid and
continue to cook for 3–5 minutes until the sauce has reduced
and thickened. Season to taste.

Speedy suppers

Pan fried chicken with peas and bacon

Serves 2
273 calories per serving
Takes 20 minutes

2 x 150 g (5½ oz) skinless boneless chicken breasts

calorie controlled cooking spray

2 x 25 g (1 oz) lean back bacon rashers, chopped

4 spring onions, chopped roughly

150 ml (5 fl oz) chicken stock

100 g (3½ oz) frozen peas

1 Little Gem lettuce, shredded roughly

salt and freshly ground black pepper

Based on a French recipe for braised peas with lettuce, this dish is bursting with flavour. Serve with 200 g (7 oz) of cooked potato, mashed with 2 tablespoons of skimmed milk.

1 Season the chicken breasts. Spray a large, lidded, non stick frying pan with the cooking spray and brown the chicken breasts for 1 minute. Turn the chicken, add the bacon to the pan and fry for 1½ minutes.

2 Stir in the spring onions and cook for 30 seconds until bright green. Pour in the chicken stock and bring to a simmer. Cover the pan, reduce the heat and simmer for 10 minutes.

3 Stir in the frozen peas and lettuce, re-cover the pan and cook for 3–4 minutes until the peas are tender and the lettuce has wilted.

Simple poached chicken with parsley sauce

Serves 2

302 calories per serving

Takes 30 minutes

❄

400 ml (14 fl oz) chicken stock

2 bay leaves

4 fresh thyme sprigs

2 x 150 g (5½ oz) skinless boneless chicken breasts

1 large leek, sliced diagonally

2 carrots, peeled and sliced diagonally

2 courgettes, sliced diagonally

3 tablespoons half fat crème fraîche

3 tablespoons chopped fresh parsley

salt and freshly ground black pepper

Poaching the chicken in stock adds to the flavour of the parsley sauce.

1 Put the stock, bay leaves and thyme in a large lidded pan and bring up to boiling point. Reduce the heat, put the chicken breasts in the pan, cover with the lid and simmer for 10 minutes.

2 Add the leek and carrots. Simmer, covered, for 8 minutes. Stir in the courgettes and simmer, uncovered, for another 3 minutes or until the chicken is cooked (check by inserting a skewer into the thickest part of the chicken – if it is cooked the juices should run clear) and the vegetables are tender.

3 Using a slotted spoon, remove the chicken and vegetables, divide them between two shallow bowls and keep warm. Remove the bay leaves and thyme from the pan and discard. Discard all but 150 ml (5 fl oz) of the cooking liquid and then add the crème fraîche and parsley to the pan. Warm through, stirring, until the sauce has thickened slightly. Season, pour over the chicken and vegetables and serve.

Cheesy chicken penne with rocket

Serves 4
396 calories per serving
Takes 20 minutes

250 g (9 oz) dried penne
175 g (6 oz) broccoli, broken into small florets
calorie controlled cooking spray
300 g (10½ oz) skinless boneless chicken breasts, cut into small pieces
3 tablespoons pesto sauce
75 g (2¾ oz) low fat soft cheese
40 g (1½ oz) wild rocket

Serve with a fresh tomato salad.

1 Bring a saucepan of water to the boil, add the pasta and cook for 10–12 minutes or according to the packet instructions, adding the broccoli for the last 3 minutes of cooking time.

2 Heat a non stick frying pan and spray with the cooking spray. Stir fry the chicken for about 8 minutes over a medium heat until golden brown and cooked through.

3 Drain the pasta and broccoli, reserving a little of the cooking water. Return to the pan and mix in the pesto, soft cheese and 4 tablespoons of the cooking water until evenly coated.

4 Stir in the chicken and rocket and serve immediately in warmed bowls.

Italian grilled chicken with sage and beans

Serves 2
347 calories per serving
Takes 20 minutes
❄ (beans only)

2 x 150 g (5½ oz) skinless
  boneless chicken breasts
calorie controlled cooking
  spray
2 teaspoons dried herbes de
  Provence or Mediterranean
  herbs
1 large onion, chopped finely
1 garlic clove, chopped finely
a small bunch of fresh sage,
  chopped
1 bay leaf
400 g can cannellini, pinto,
  kidney or borlotti beans,
  drained and rinsed
grated zest and juice of a
  lemon
150 g (5½ oz) green beans,
  trimmed and cut into 2.5 cm
  (1 inch) lengths
100 ml (3½ fl oz) vegetable
  stock
salt and freshly ground black
  pepper

*Cannellini beans cooked like this with sage are well known
in Tuscany where they generally accompany roast meat.*

1 Preheat the grill to medium-high. Slice the chicken breasts
in half horizontally to make four thinner fillets. Season and
spray with the cooking spray and then sprinkle with the dried
herbs. Grill for 3–4 minutes, or until golden brown on each
side. Remove to a plate and set aside.

2 Spray a large lidded saucepan with the cooking spray and
stir fry the onion and garlic with a few tablespoons of water,
until softened. Add the sage and bay leaf and then stir in the
canned beans, lemon juice, green beans and stock.

3 Place the grilled chicken on top of the bean mixture and
cover the pan. Leave to steam for 5 minutes until the chicken
is cooked through and the green beans are tender. Serve
scattered with the lemon zest.

Sticky apricot chicken

Serves 2
235 calories per serving
Takes 25 minutes

2 x 150 g (5½ oz) skinless
  boneless chicken breasts
2 tablespoons apricot jam
1 tablespoon tomato ketchup
1 tablespoon lemon juice
1 teaspoon smooth mustard
  (Dijon or English)
a pinch of cayenne pepper
  or chilli powder
salt

*Apricot jam gives this barbecue style sauce sweetness,
then there's a gentle kick from the mustard and cayenne
pepper. Serve with steamed broccoli and 150 g (5½ oz)
new potatoes.*

1 Preheat the oven to Gas Mark 7/220°C/fan oven 200°C. Line
a roasting tin with foil or non stick baking parchment to stop
the glaze sticking to the tin.

2 Lightly slash the chicken on both sides and place in the
roasting tin.

3 Mix the jam with the ketchup, lemon juice and mustard
and season with salt and a pinch of cayenne pepper or chilli
powder. Brush half the glaze over the chicken and roast for
10 minutes.

4 Turn the chicken over and brush with the remaining glaze.
Cook for a further 10 minutes until cooked through and
deliciously sticky.

Chicken and cashew nuts

Serves 4
282 calories per serving
Takes 30 minutes

1 teaspoon sunflower oil

40 g (1½ oz) cashew nuts, halved

350 g (12 oz) skinless boneless chicken breasts, diced

2 teaspoons sesame oil

2 carrots, peeled and cut into thin batons

150 g (5½ oz) baby corn, cut into thirds

100 g (3½ oz) mange tout, halved

2 garlic cloves, sliced

a bunch of spring onions, cut into 2.5 cm (1 inch) lengths, reserving some, sliced finely, for garnishing

2 tablespoons soy sauce

1 tablespoon dry sherry

300 ml (10 fl oz) chicken stock

1 tablespoon cornflour

Toasted cashew nuts give this colourful stir fry an extra crunch. As with all stir fried dishes, make sure everything is prepared before you actually start to cook, as the pace is fast and furious. Serve with 60 g (2 oz) of dried long grain rice per person, cooked according to the packet instructions.

1 Heat the sunflower oil in a lidded wok or large, lidded, non stick frying pan and gently brown the cashew nuts. Remove with a slotted spoon and set aside.

2 Coat the chicken in the sesame oil, tip into the hot wok or frying pan and cook for 3 minutes, stirring occasionally, until browned.

3 Add the carrots, baby corn, mange tout and garlic and stir fry for 2 minutes.

4 Stir in the spring onions, soy sauce and sherry and cook for 1 minute.

5 Return the cashew nuts to the wok, add the chicken stock, cover and simmer for 5 minutes.

6 Blend the cornflour with 1 tablespoon of cold water and stir into the sauce until slightly thickened. Serve immediately, garnished with the reserved spring onions.

Grilled chicken with orange and ginger

Serves 4
267 calories per serving
Takes 15 minutes to prepare,
15 minutes to cook

**4 x 165 g (5¾ oz) skinless
boneless chicken breasts**
**2 tablespoons stir fry oil or
sesame oil**
1 large leek, shredded
**1 carrot, peeled and sliced
finely**
**100 g (3½ oz) mange tout or
sugar snap peas**
juice of an orange
**2.5 cm (1 inch) fresh root
ginger, finely grated**
1 teaspoon Chinese five spice
**salt and freshly ground black
pepper**

To serve
1 teaspoon sesame seeds
a few fresh coriander sprigs
finely grated zest of an orange

*A simple chicken dish tastes really special when served
with interesting flavours.*

1 Preheat the grill and cover the grill pan with foil. Arrange the
chicken breasts on the grill pan and brush with a little of the oil.
Grill under a medium-high heat for about 5–6 minutes on each
side, or until tender. (There should be no trace of pink when
tested with a sharp knife.)

2 Meanwhile, heat the remaining oil in a wok or non stick
frying pan and stir fry the leek, carrot and mange tout or sugar
snap peas for about 3 minutes, until cooked yet still crunchy.

3 Mix together the orange juice, ginger and Chinese five spice.
Add to the vegetables and stir until heated. Season to taste.

4 Divide the vegetable mixture between four warmed serving
plates and top with the chicken. Scatter with the sesame
seeds, fresh coriander and orange zest and serve at once.

Lime and ginger chicken

Serves 2
294 calories per serving
Takes 25 minutes
❄

1 teaspoon sunflower oil

225 g (8 oz) skinless boneless chicken breasts, sliced thinly

1 red chilli, de-seeded and chopped finely

1 garlic clove, crushed

2.5 cm (1 inch) fresh root ginger, grated

finely grated zest of a lime

2 tablespoons light soy sauce

1 teaspoon runny honey

175 g (6 oz) white cabbage, shredded

100 g (3½ oz) mange tout, halved

6 spring onions, sliced into thin strips

75 g (2¾ oz) canned water chestnuts, drained and sliced

150 g (5½ oz) carrots, peeled and cut into ribbons

150 ml (5 fl oz) chicken stock

1 teaspoon cornflour

2 tablespoons fresh lime juice

The vibrant fresh flavours of ginger and lime bring this tasty stir fry to life.

1 Heat the sunflower oil in a wok or large non stick frying pan and add the chicken. Stir fry for 4–5 minutes to seal it on all sides. Add the chilli, garlic, ginger, lime zest, soy sauce and honey and stir fry until it is all bubbling.

2 Add the cabbage, mange tout, spring onions and water chestnuts and stir fry for 2 minutes. Add the carrot ribbons to the pan.

3 Pour in the stock and bring to the boil. Cook over a high heat for 3 minutes. Mix the cornflour with the lime juice to make a paste and stir this into the pan. Cook, stirring, until the juices thicken a little and then serve at once.

Coronation chicken

Serves 2
339 calories per serving
Takes 20 minutes

100 g (3½ oz) 0% fat Greek
  yogurt or low fat natural
  yogurt
1 teaspoon mild curry powder
2 teaspoons chopped fresh
  coriander or mint (optional)
1 banana, sliced
40 g (1½ oz) ready to eat dried
  apricots, chopped
15 g (½ oz) raisins or sultanas
225 g (8 oz) cooked skinless
  boneless chicken breast,
  sliced
crisp lettuce leaves
cucumber slices
salt and freshly ground black
  pepper
fresh coriander and mint
  leaves, to garnish (optional)

This tastes superb. Serve with a side dish of halved cherry tomatoes and chopped spring onions, with fat free dressing.

1 In a large bowl, mix together the yogurt, curry powder and coriander or mint, if using.

2 Add the banana, apricots, raisins or sultanas. Mix in the chicken, stirring gently to coat in the curry sauce. Season to taste.

3 Arrange some lettuce leaves and cucumber slices on two serving plates and share out the chicken mixture between them. Garnish with a few coriander or mint leaves, if using. Serve at once.

Provençal chicken

Serves 4
284 calories per serving
Takes 30 minutes

4 x 175 g (6 oz) skinless boneless chicken breasts

calorie controlled cooking spray

2 teaspoons paprika

For the Provençal salsa

1 small cucumber, cut lengthways into quarters, de-seeded and cut into small chunks

3 large vine-ripened tomatoes, quartered, de-seeded and cut into small chunks

1 small yellow pepper, de-seeded and cut into small chunks

20 stoned black olives, halved

½ red onion, sliced thinly into rings

4 tablespoons chopped fresh flat leaf parsley

juice of ½ a lemon

2 teaspoons extra virgin olive oil

salt and freshly ground black pepper

Chargrilling gives food a wonderful smoky barbecue flavour without the need to use too much oil. If you don't have a griddle pan, simply grill the chicken for 8–10 minutes on each side in step 1.

1 Spray the chicken with the cooking spray and sprinkle the paprika over each side. Heat a griddle pan until hot. Reduce the heat to medium and griddle the chicken, two breasts at a time, for about 6 minutes on each side until cooked through. Keep warm.

2 Meanwhile, put the cucumber, tomatoes, pepper, olives, onion and parsley in a serving bowl. Pour over the lemon juice and oil, season well and stir until combined. Serve the chicken with the Provençal salsa by the side.

Thai chicken stir fry

Serves 1
253 calories per serving
Takes 15 minutes

calorie controlled cooking
   spray
165 g (5¾ oz) skinless
   boneless chicken breast,
   sliced very thinly
1 carrot, peeled and cut into
   matchstick shapes
2 spring onions, sliced
½ red pepper, de-seeded and
   thinly sliced
½ teaspoon cornflour
1 tablespoon soy sauce
¼ teaspoon grated fresh root
   ginger

A tasty yet simple dish that can be put together quickly for a single supper.

1 Heat a non stick frying pan, spray with the cooking spray and stir fry the chicken and vegetables for 5 minutes.

2 Mix the cornflour to a paste with 4 tablespoons of water, stir together with the rest of the ingredients and add to the pan.

3 Mix in well and cook for 2–3 minutes, stirring constantly.

Tip... For extra flavour and heat, add 1 tablespoon of chopped fresh coriander and ½ red chilli, de-seeded and chopped finely.

BBQ chicken with home made coleslaw

Serves 4
250 calories per serving
Takes 30 minutes

2 tablespoons tomato ketchup
2 tablespoons balsamic
  vinegar
1 tablespoon runny honey
4 x 150 g (5½ oz) skinless
  boneless chicken breasts
calorie controlled cooking
  spray

For the coleslaw
150 g (5½ oz) red cabbage,
  grated
2 carrots, peeled and grated
2 spring onions, sliced finely
3 tablespoons low fat natural
  yogurt
2 tablespoons reduced fat
  mayonnaise
juice of ¼ of a lemon
1 heaped teaspoon wholegrain
  mustard
salt and freshly ground black
  pepper

A quick and easy dish with plenty of flavour.

1 Preheat the grill to high and cover the grill pan with foil. In a bowl, mix together the ketchup, vinegar and honey. Make 2–3 cuts in the top of each chicken breast and place them in a shallow dish. Spoon the marinade over the chicken and leave for 5 minutes.

2 Place the chicken on the grill pan and spray with the cooking spray. Grill for about 15 minutes until cooked through, turning once and spooning over the barbecue sauce when needed.

3 Meanwhile, to make the coleslaw, put the cabbage, carrots and spring onions into a bowl. Mix together the yogurt, mayonnaise, lemon juice, mustard and 1 tablespoon of water. Season and pour over the vegetables. Stir until combined. Serve the chicken on top of the coleslaw.

Chinese chicken

Serves 4
207 calories per serving
Takes 30 minutes

4 x 150 g (5½ oz) skinless
  boneless chicken breasts,
  cut into small chunks
1 garlic clove, crushed
2.5 cm (1 inch) fresh root
  ginger, grated
2 tablespoons soy sauce
juice of ½ a lemon
calorie controlled cooking
  spray
1 green pepper, de-seeded and
  sliced
1 carrot, peeled and sliced
  finely
½ red chilli, de-seeded and
  sliced finely
1 onion, sliced
100 ml (3½ fl oz) white wine
  vinegar
2 tablespoons artificial
  sweetener
100 ml (3½ fl oz) passata
2 spring onions, sliced finely

Serve with a portion of egg fried rice (see Tip).

1 Put the chicken in a non metallic bowl and mix with the garlic, ginger, 1 tablespoon of soy sauce and lemon juice.

2 Heat a wok or non stick frying pan until hot. Spray with the cooking spray and stir fry the chicken for 5 minutes until starting to brown. Add the pepper, carrot, chilli and onion and stir fry for a further 3 minutes.

3 Add the vinegar, sweetener, passata and remaining soy sauce. Cook for 2 minutes until starting to thicken. Sprinkle over the spring onions and serve.

Tip... To make fried rice for four people, heat a wok or non stick frying pan until very hot and then spray with calorie controlled cooking spray. Add 350 g (12 oz) of cooked cold brown rice and 3 finely chopped spring onions and cook for 2 minutes, stirring. Add 1 lightly beaten egg and 75 g (2¾ oz) of petit pois. Cook for 2 minutes, stirring to break up the egg. Transfer to a serving dish and keep warm.

Simply special

Rosemary and lemon chicken

Serves 4

569 calories per serving

Takes 25 minutes to prepare,
30 minutes to cook

8 x 85 g (3 oz) skinless
boneless chicken thighs,
cut into bite size pieces

2 unwaxed lemons, halved

950 g (2 lb 2 oz) potatoes,
peeled and cut into 4 cm
(1½ inch) cubes

6 garlic cloves, halved
lengthways

2 onions, sliced

10 fresh rosemary sprigs,
2 reserved to garnish

calorie controlled cooking
spray

salt and freshly ground black
pepper

*This is a fantastically fragrant chicken and potato bake
from Italy. Serve with steamed green beans.*

1 Put the chicken pieces into a bowl, season and then squeeze
over the lemon halves. Slice one of the squeezed lemon halves
into thin slivers and add these to the bowl too.

2 Bring a large saucepan of water to the boil, add the potatoes
and cook for 4 minutes only. Drain.

3 Preheat the oven to Gas Mark 7/220°C/fan oven 200°C.
Put all the ingredients into a roasting tin, spray with the calorie
controlled cooking spray, lightly season and toss together.
Bake for 30 minutes, turning every now and then until crispy
and golden and cooked through. Serve garnished with the
reserved fresh rosemary sprigs.

Tarragon chicken with lemon braised potatoes

Serves 2
323 calories per serving
Takes 10 minutes to prepare,
25 minutes to cook

300 g (10½ oz) baby new potatoes, halved
300 ml (10 fl oz) chicken or vegetable stock
grated zest and juice of ½ a lemon
2 tablespoons chopped fresh tarragon
3 tablespoons chopped fresh parsley
calorie controlled cooking spray
2 x 150 g (5½ oz) skinless boneless chicken breasts
calorie controlled cooking spray
16 cherry tomatoes on the vine
¼ teaspoon granulated sugar
salt and freshly ground black pepper

This is an ideal recipe when you want a special meal for two that is really quick to prepare. Add some steamed broccoli to complete the meal.

1 Preheat the oven to Gas Mark 6/200°C/ fan oven 180°C. Place the potatoes in a large lidded saucepan with the stock, 1 tablespoon of lemon juice and ½ teaspoon of lemon zest. Bring to the boil and simmer, covered, for 15 minutes until tender.

2 Meanwhile, mix the remaining lemon zest with the tarragon and 2 tablespoons of parsley on a plate. Spray the chicken breasts with a little cooking spray and season them lightly. Roll the chicken in the herb mixture to coat completely and place in a lightly greased roasting tin. Drizzle the rest of the lemon juice over the chicken and cook in the oven for 10 minutes.

3 Add the tomatoes to the roasting tin with the chicken, lightly spray with the cooking spray and sprinkle with the sugar. Return the roasting tin to the oven for 10 minutes, or until the chicken juices run clear when the thickest part of the breast is pierced with a sharp knife or skewer.

4 When the potatoes are tender, remove the lid and increase the heat under the pan. Reduce the liquid for about 10 minutes or until it has almost all evaporated and you are left with about 2 tablespoons of syrupy juices. Toss the potatoes in the juices to glaze and scatter with the remaining parsley. Serve with the chicken and roasted tomatoes.

Chicken breasts with Feta

Serves 2

304 calories per serving

Takes 15 minutes to prepare,
20–25 minutes to cook

40 g (1½ oz) Feta cheese

5 black or green olives, stoned
and chopped finely

1 teaspoon olive oil

2 x 165 g (5¾ oz) skinless
boneless chicken breasts

1 aubergine, sliced

2 beefsteak tomatoes, sliced

1 garlic clove, sliced thickly

calorie controlled cooking
spray

salt and freshly ground black
pepper

This is delicious served with 150 g (5½ oz) of boiled new potatoes per person and fresh watercress.

1 Preheat the oven to Gas Mark 6/200°C/fan oven 180°C.

2 Make the stuffing by mashing together the cheese, olives and olive oil with a fork to make a stiff paste.

3 Carefully cut a pocket in the side of each chicken breast and divide the stuffing mixture between them. Close the pockets and secure with cocktail sticks.

4 Layer the aubergine and tomato slices in a shallow ovenproof baking dish, slipping the slices of garlic between them. Place the stuffed chicken breasts on top, spray with the cooking spray and season.

5 Roast for 35–40 minutes until the chicken is cooked. Test with a sharp knife to make sure that the juices run clear.

Tips... If you like, replace the fresh tomatoes with a 400 g can of chopped tomatoes for a runnier sauce.

The stuffing mixture can also be whizzed together in a blender.

Rich red chicken with rosemary and cherry tomatoes

Serves 4

294 calories per serving

Takes 50 minutes to prepare,
50 minutes to cook

❄

4 onions, quartered

4 teaspoons olive oil

300 g (10½ oz) skinless
boneless chicken breasts

2 garlic cloves, crushed

3 teaspoons fresh rosemary,
chopped

2 tablespoons sun-dried
tomato purée

100 ml (3½ fl oz) red wine

2 teaspoons plain flour

450 ml (16 fl oz) chicken stock

350 g (12 oz) small flat
mushrooms

2 tablespoons wholegrain
mustard

225 g (8 oz) cherry tomatoes

salt and freshly ground black
pepper

fresh flat leaf parsley, to
garnish

*A bright cheery recipe that resonates with summer
flavours.*

1 Preheat the oven to Gas Mark 4/180°C/fan oven 160°C.
Heat a large non stick frying pan until hot and add the onions
with 2 teaspoons of oil. Reduce the heat and cook for
10 minutes, stirring, until the onions are just beginning to
soften and turn golden. Using a slotted spoon, transfer them
to a large ovenproof casserole dish with a tight fitting lid.

2 Add the remaining oil and the chicken to the pan. Cook on
one side for 5 minutes until the meat seals and colours slightly.
Add the garlic and rosemary, turn the chicken over and cook for
a further 5 minutes. Transfer the chicken to the casserole dish.

3 Stir the tomato purée and wine into the garlic and rosemary.
Cook for 3–4 minutes to reduce slightly and then blend in the
flour. Cook, stirring, for a further 3–4 minutes until smooth.
Stir in the stock, bring to the boil and pour the mixture over the
chicken. Cover the casserole dish and bake for 50 minutes.

4 Meanwhile, wipe out the frying pan with kitchen towel and
dry fry the mushrooms over a gentle heat until they begin to
soften and release a little moisture. Continue to cook gently
for 5 minutes.

5 Stir the mushrooms, mustard and tomatoes into the
casserole and season to taste. Return to the oven, uncovered,
for 10 minutes or until the tomatoes are just tender. Serve,
garnished with the parsley.

Creamy garlic chicken with roasted tomatoes

Serves 2

258 calories per serving

Takes 5 minutes to prepare,
20 minutes to cook

2 x 165 g (5¾ oz) skinless
boneless chicken breasts

40 g (1½ oz) Boursin light

2 slices Parma ham

calorie controlled cooking
spray

175 g (6 oz) cherry tomatoes
on the vine

1 teaspoon fresh thyme leaves

2 tablespoons balsamic
vinegar

salt and freshly ground black
pepper

A luxurious recipe that is very quick to prepare, making it ideal for a special occasion. Serve with fine green beans and 150 g (5½ oz) new potatoes.

1 Preheat the oven to Gas Mark 6/200°C/fan oven 180°C.

2 Cut a pocket in the side of each chicken breast and stuff with the Boursin. Season and then wrap a slice of Parma ham around each one. Place in a roasting tin and spray with the cooking spray. Roast for 10 minutes.

3 Remove the tin from the oven, add the tomatoes on the vine and spray them with the cooking spray. Sprinkle the tomatoes with thyme and seasoning and drizzle with 1 tablespoon of balsamic vinegar. Roast for a further 8 minutes.

4 Lift the chicken and tomatoes out on to warmed plates, leaving behind any cheese that has oozed out. Add the remaining balsamic vinegar and 1 tablespoon of water to the tin. Place over a medium heat and whisk for 30 seconds to form a sauce. Pour over the chicken and serve.

Coq au vin

Serves 4

433 calories per serving

Takes 15 minutes to prepare,
1¼ hours to cook

❄

calorie controlled cooking
  spray
4 x 165 g (5¾ oz) skinless
  chicken legs
2 x 165 g (5¾ oz) skinless
  boneless chicken breasts,
  halved
8 shallots, 4 whole and
  4 chopped finely
4 carrots, peeled and cut into
  batons
1 garlic clove, crushed
1 tablespoon mixed herbs
1 tablespoon tomato purée
500 ml (18 fl oz) red wine
150 g (5½ oz) baby chestnut
  mushrooms
2 courgettes, sliced
2 bay leaves
500 g (1 lb 2 oz) small
  potatoes, scrubbed
salt and freshly ground black
  pepper

A wonderful version of this classic dish.

1 Heat a large, lidded, non stick pan and spray with the
cooking spray. Gently fry the chicken pieces until lightly
browned. Remove and put to one side.

2 Re-spray the pan, add the chopped and whole shallots and
the carrots and gently fry for 3 minutes. Add the garlic, herbs,
tomato purée and wine and season. Stir, bring to the boil and
let it all bubble for 2 minutes.

3 Return the chicken pieces to the pan with all the remaining
ingredients except the potatoes.

4 Stir well, reduce the heat to a gentle simmer, cover and cook
for 1 hour, turning the chicken pieces over after 35 minutes.

5 Meanwhile, bring a saucepan of water to the boil, add the
potatoes and cook for 8–10 minutes until tender. Drain, allow
to cool and slice.

6 About 10 minutes before serving, heat a non stick frying pan
and spray with the cooking spray. Sauté the sliced potatoes
until golden.

7 To serve, place half a breast and a chicken leg on each of
four warmed plates. Add some of the casserole vegetables and
the sauté potatoes. Pour over the wine gravy.

Tip... You can also cook this dish in the oven at Gas Mark 4/
180°C/fan oven 160°C. Place it in an ovenproof dish at the
end of stage 3 and pop it in the oven for 1½ hours.

Caribbean chicken

Serves 2
444 calories per serving
Takes 20 minutes to prepare,
  1 hour to cook

calorie controlled cooking
  spray
2 x 150 g (5½ oz) skinless
  boneless chicken breasts
1 onion, chopped
½ green pepper, de-seeded
  and chopped
2 teaspoons cornflour
2 canned pineapple rings
  in natural juice, with
  2 tablespoons juice
300 ml (10 fl oz) chicken stock
2 teaspoons tomato ketchup
2 teaspoons curry powder
salt and freshly ground black
  pepper

To serve
175 g (6 oz) dried long grain
  rice
1 banana

*This dish, with the colours and flavours of the Caribbean,
is a favourite with everyone.*

1 Preheat the oven to Gas Mark 4/180°C/fan oven 160°C. Heat
a large non stick frying pan, spray with the cooking spray and
brown the chicken breasts. Remove them to a large ovenproof
dish.

2 Spray the frying pan with the cooking spray again, add the
onion and pepper and lightly fry. Add them to the chicken.

3 Blend the cornflour with the pineapple juice. Pour the stock
into the frying pan and then add the pineapple rings, cornflour
mixture, ketchup and curry powder. Season. Bring the mixture
to the boil and pour it over the chicken.

4 Bake for 1 hour or until the chicken is cooked.

5 Meanwhile, bring a saucepan of water to the boil, add the
rice and cook according to the packet instructions.

6 Slice the banana in half lengthways, cut it into pieces and
stir into the chicken sauce just before serving. Divide the sauce
into two equal portions and serve with the chicken and rice.

Mushroom and tarragon stuffed chicken

Serves 4

195 calories per serving

Takes 25 minutes to prepare,
30–35 minutes to cook

calorie controlled cooking
spray

1 small leek, chopped finely

1 small courgette, chopped
finely

1 garlic clove, crushed

100 g (3½ oz) mushrooms,
chopped finely

a small bunch of fresh
tarragon, woody stems
removed and leaves chopped

4 x 150 g (5½ oz) skinless
boneless chicken breasts

2 teaspoons soy sauce

150 g (5½ oz) low fat natural
yogurt

salt and freshly ground black
pepper

*Serve with roasted cherry tomatoes on the vine, seasoned
and sprinkled with balsamic vinegar.*

1 Soak eight cocktail sticks in water for 10 minutes to prevent
them from burning. Preheat the oven to Gas Mark 6/200°C/fan
oven 180°C.

2 Heat a large non stick frying pan and spray with the cooking
spray. Add the leek, courgette, garlic and mushrooms, season
and cook for 5 minutes. Remove from the heat and stir in the
tarragon.

3 Place the chicken breasts between two sheets of baking
parchment and beat to an even thickness with a rolling pin.
Season, spread 1–2 tablespoons of the tarragon mixture
over each breast and roll up, folding in the ends. Secure with
the soaked cocktail sticks. Set aside any remaining tarragon
mixture.

4 Place the chicken on a non stick baking tray. Bake for
30–35 minutes, until the juices run clear when pierced with
a knife. Remove the cocktail sticks. Slice each roll diagonally
into three or four pieces.

5 To make the sauce, heat the remaining tarragon mixture and
then add the soy sauce and yogurt. Warm through but do not
boil. Check the seasoning and serve with the chicken.

Baked lemon spring chicken

Serves 4

237 calories per serving

Takes 15 minutes to prepare,
40 minutes to cook

**4 x 165 g (5¾ oz) skinless
boneless chicken breasts**

**4 spring onions, chopped
finely**

2 garlic cloves, crushed

**2 small red chillies, de-seeded
and chopped finely (optional)**

**grated zest and juice of
2 lemons**

4 teaspoons olive oil

**salt and freshly ground black
pepper**

*A fresh tasting quick chicken dish. Serve with courgettes
and steamed al dente baby carrots.*

1 Preheat the oven to Gas Mark 4/180°C/fan oven 160°C. Put
the chicken breasts in a large ovenproof baking dish lined with
foil. Scatter over the remaining ingredients and fold the foil up
to enclose the chicken.

2 Bake for 40 minutes. Unwrap the foil for the last 10 minutes
to allow the chicken to brown.

Spanish chicken

Serves 4

309 calories per serving

Takes 30 minutes to prepare,
45 minutes to cook

❄

4 skinless chicken legs
(660 g/1 lb 7 oz total
weight), each cut into two at
the joint

calorie controlled cooking
spray

2 onions, sliced

2 red peppers, de-seeded and
sliced

2 garlic cloves, crushed

400 g can chopped tomatoes

50 g (1¾ oz) stoned black
olives in brine, drained and
halved

1 teaspoon cayenne pepper

1 tablespoon tomato purée

1 teaspoon dried mixed herbs

150 ml (5 fl oz) chicken stock

1 orange, cut into eight
segments

salt and freshly ground black
pepper

Bring some Spanish sun to your plate with this very easy and colourful dish. It is fantastic with plain white rice or couscous and whole green beans.

1 Season the chicken joints thoroughly. Heat a large, lidded, non stick pan and spray with the cooking spray. Add the chicken and brown on both sides for a couple of minutes, then remove and put to one side.

2 Spray the pan with the cooking spray again, add the onions, peppers and garlic and cook for 5 minutes until soft. Add all the remaining ingredients except the orange and the chicken, stir well and bring back to a simmer.

3 Once the tomato mixture is simmering again, put the chicken joints back into the pan and position the orange segments around them. Cover the pan and simmer gently for 40 minutes, or until the chicken is cooked through.

4 Serve on four warmed plates.

Chicken Maryland

Serves 4
573 calories per serving
Takes 35 minutes

2 level tablespoons plain flour
4 x 175 g (6 oz) skinless boneless chicken breasts
1 egg, beaten
4 medium slices fresh bread, made into breadcrumbs
calorie controlled cooking spray
2 bananas, peeled
2 teaspoons runny honey, warmed
juice of ½ a lemon
salt and freshly ground black pepper

For the sweetcorn fitters
100 g (3½ oz) plain flour
1 egg
150 ml (5 fl oz) skimmed milk
310 g can sweetcorn, drained

Chicken Maryland is nearly impossible to find in restaurants now, so make it at home for friends. It is delicious served with tomato ketchup.

1 Sprinkle the flour on to a plate and season. Coat each chicken breast in the flour, dip in the egg and finally coat in the breadcrumbs.

2 Heat a large non stick frying pan and spray with the cooking spray. Fry the chicken for 5 minutes on each side until golden brown and cooked through. Keep warm while you prepare the bananas and make the sweetcorn fritters.

3 Preheat the grill to medium. Slice the bananas in half lengthways and brush with the honey and lemon juice. Grill for 4 minutes until golden.

4 Make the fritters by beating together the flour, egg, milk and seasoning and then stirring in the sweetcorn. Spray a non stick frying pan with the cooking spray and fry spoonfuls of the batter for 2–3 minutes on each side, turning with a fish slice. Put on a plate and keep warm with the chicken and bananas until all the fritters are cooked.

5 Serve the chicken with a banana half and 2 or 3 corn fritters each.

Tip... Keep the different elements warm in a low oven until ready to serve.

Lemon chicken with leeks and rice

Serves 4

363 calories per serving

Takes 15 minutes to prepare,
   30 minutes to cook

1 tablespoon olive oil

1 leek, chopped finely

125 g (4½ oz) dried risotto rice

600 ml (20 fl oz) hot chicken
   stock

1 tablespoon plain flour

1 teaspoon ground ginger

finely grated zest and juice of
   a lemon

4 x 165 g (5¾ oz) skinless
   boneless chicken breasts

2 tablespoons light soy sauce

50 g (1¾ oz) frozen peas

salt and freshly ground black
   pepper

To serve
lemon slices
fresh herbs (optional)

Lemon and ginger-flavoured chicken breasts on a bed of creamy risotto taste amazing – you must try them.

1 Heat the olive oil in a large non stick frying pan and add the leek and rice. Cook gently, stirring, until the rice looks translucent – about 3 minutes. Add the stock a ladleful at a time, allowing the rice to absorb the liquid before adding the next ladleful.

2 Meanwhile, mix together the flour, ginger and lemon zest and season. Roll the chicken breasts in this mixture.

3 Preheat the grill. Mix together the lemon juice and soy sauce. Arrange the chicken on the grill pan and brush with the lemon juice mixture. Cook for about 8 minutes on each side.

4 Check that the rice is cooked – it should be creamy and tender. Add the peas and cook for 2–3 minutes to heat them through.

5 Pile the rice on to warmed serving plates and arrange the chicken breasts on top. Garnish with lemon slices and herbs, if using, and serve.

Tip... Make sure that you use a genuine risotto rice for the best results. Long grain rice will not work because it does not absorb enough liquid to become soft and creamy.

Grilled chicken with grapes

Serves 4
200 calories per serving
Takes 25 minutes +
  marinating

200 ml (7 fl oz) red grape juice
1 small onion or 2 shallots,
  chopped finely
a small bunch of fresh parsley,
  chopped finely
juice of a lemon
4 x 150 g (5½ oz) skinless
  boneless chicken breasts
100 g (3½ oz) red grapes,
  halved
salt and freshly ground black
  pepper

*A slightly unusual but delicious combination of flavours.
Serve with 60 g (2 oz) of dried basmati rice per person,
cooked according to the packet instructions.*

1 Put the grape juice, onion or shallots, parsley and lemon juice in a large bowl and add the chicken. Season and stir until the chicken is thoroughly coated in the marinade. Chill and leave to marinate for a minimum of 30 minutes, but preferably overnight.

2 Preheat the grill to medium-high. Take the chicken out of the marinade and grill for 4–8 minutes on each side, until cooked through and golden.

3 Meanwhile, heat the marinade with the grapes until boiling and then turn down the heat and simmer for a few minutes to reduce the sauce down a little.

4 Serve the chicken with the hot marinade sauce.

Chicken parcels with vegetable ribbons

Serves 4

155 calories per serving

Takes 20 minutes to prepare,
30 minutes to cook

1 teaspoon paprika
1 teaspoon Chinese five spice
½ teaspoon salt
1 garlic clove, crushed
**2.5 cm (1 inch) fresh root
ginger, cut into very thin
strands**
**4 x 100 g (3½ oz) skinless
boneless chicken breasts**
175 g (6 oz) carrots, peeled
175 g (6 oz) courgettes
**4 spring onions, sliced into
long thin strips**
4 tablespoons light soy sauce
1 teaspoon sesame oil

*Because of the strong flavours in this recipe, you only need
a very simple accompaniment, such as 60 g (2 oz) of dried
jasmine rice per person, cooked according to the packet
instructions, or 200 g (7 oz) of baby new potatoes.*

1 Preheat the oven to Gas Mark 5/190°C/fan oven 170°C.

2 Cut a sheet of non stick baking parchment into four 30 cm
(12 inch) squares. Lay them out, side by side, on a clean work
surface.

3 Mix together the paprika, Chinese five spice, salt, garlic and
ginger. Rub this mixture into the chicken breasts.

4 Place one chicken breast in the centre of each sheet of
baking parchment.

5 Using a swivel head potato peeler, peel the carrots and
courgettes into thin ribbons. Place the ribbons in a large bowl,
followed by the spring onions and soy sauce, and mix well.

6 Pile equal amounts of the vegetable ribbons over each
chicken breast and drizzle over the sesame oil and any soy
sauce left in the bowl. Wrap the parchment up tightly to
enclose the chicken and vegetables. Put the chicken parcels
in a roasting tin.

7 Bake for 30 minutes. Unwrap the parcels carefully on to
warmed serving plates.

Summer chicken casserole

Serves 4

676 calories per serving

Takes 10 minutes to prepare,
   1 hour to cook

calorie controlled cooking
   spray

450 g (1 lb) skinless boneless
   chicken breasts, cut into
   pieces

2 garlic cloves, sliced

12 baby onions or small
   shallots

150 ml (5 fl oz) dry white wine

1 litre (1¾ pints) chicken or
   vegetable stock

8 baby carrots, scrubbed

8 baby turnips, scrubbed and
   halved

450 g (1 lb) baby parsnips,
   scrubbed

200 g (7 oz) frozen or fresh
   peas

350 g (12 oz) dried pasta
   ribbons

4 tablespoons half fat crème
   fraîche

salt and freshly ground black
   pepper

This is elegant enough, served with plain ribbon pasta, to serve up at a dinner party.

1 Heat a large flameproof casserole or non stick pan over a medium heat and spray with the cooking spray. Add the chicken, brown on all sides, season and remove to a plate.

2 Put the garlic and onions or shallots in the casserole or pan and fry over a medium heat until softened and golden – about 4 minutes. Add the wine and scrape the bottom of the pan with a wooden spoon for 1 minute.

3 Return the chicken to the casserole or pan and add the stock. Bring to the boil and then simmer for 45 minutes. Add the vegetables to the pan and simmer for a further 15 minutes.

4 Meanwhile, bring a saucepan of water to the boil, add the pasta and cook according to the packet instructions. Drain.

5 Stir the crème fraîche into the casserole and check the seasoning before serving with the pasta.

Chicken with ratatouille

Serves 2

307 calories per serving

Takes 15 minutes to prepare,
20 minutes to cook

❄ (up to 1 month)

**60 g (2 oz) low fat soft cheese
with garlic and herbs**

1 spring onion, chopped

**2 x 165 g (5¾ oz) skinless
boneless chicken breasts**

600 ml (20 fl oz) chicken stock

For the ratatouille

**calorie controlled cooking
spray**

1 small onion, chopped

**1 red pepper, de-seeded and
chopped**

1 courgette, sliced

227 g can chopped tomatoes

**salt and freshly ground black
pepper**

*Stuffing chicken breasts helps to keep them moist and
adds extra flavour to the meat.*

1 In a small bowl, mix together the soft cheese and spring onion.

2 Wrap each chicken breast in a large piece of cling film. Apply
pressure with a rolling pin to make the breast thinner. Open the
cling film, place half the cheese mixture on the chicken breast
and roll it up. Wrap the breast up tightly in the cling film.

3 Put the chicken stock in a saucepan and bring to a simmer.
Place the stuffed wrapped breasts in the stock. Simmer for
15 minutes.

4 Meanwhile, make the ratatouille. Spray a small non stick
saucepan with the cooking spray, add the onion and pepper
and cook for 2–3 minutes before adding the remaining
ingredients. Simmer for 12–15 minutes.

5 When the chicken breasts are cooked, remove them from
the stock and leave to cool slightly before unwrapping. Slice
the chicken.

6 Divide the ratatouille and slices of chicken between two
warmed plates.

Index